Predicting Information Retrieval Performance

Synthesis Lectures on Information Concepts, Retrieval, and Services

Editor
Gary Marchionini, *University of North Carolina, Chapel Hill*

Synthesis Lectures on Information Concepts, Retrieval, and Services publishes short books on topics pertaining to information science and applications of technology to information discovery, production, distribution, and management. Potential topics include: data models, indexing theory and algorithms, classification, information architecture, information economics, privacy and identity, scholarly communication, bibliometrics and webometrics, personal information management, human information behavior, digital libraries, archives and preservation, cultural informatics, information retrieval evaluation, data fusion, relevance feedback, recommendation systems, question answering, natural language processing for retrieval, text summarization, multimedia retrieval, multilingual retrieval, and exploratory search.

Predicting Information Retrieval Performance
Robert M. Losee
2018

Framing Privacy in Digital Collections with Ethical Decision Making
Virginia Dressler
2018

Mobile Search Behaviors: An In-depth Analysis Based on Contexts, APPs, and Devices
Dan Wu and Shaobo Liang
2018

Images in Social Media: Categorization and Organization of Images and Their Collections
Susanne Ørnager and Haakon Lund
2018

Exploring Context in Information Behavior: Seeker, Situation, Surroundings, and Shared Identities
Naresh Kumar Agarwal
2017

Predicting Information Retrieval Performance

Robert M. Losee

ISBN: 978-3-031-01189-4   paperback
ISBN: 978-3-031-02317-0   ebook
ISBN: 978-3-031-00224-3   hardcover

DOI 10.1007/978-3-031-02317-0

A Publication in the Springer series
SYNTHESIS LECTURES ON INFORMATION CONCEPTS, RETRIEVAL, AND SERVICES

Lecture #65
Series Editor: Gary Marchionini, *University of North Carolina, Chapel Hill*
Series ISSN
Print 1947-945X   Electronic 1947-9468

Predicting
Information Retrieval
Performance

Robert M. Losee
University of North Carolina, Chapel Hill

SYNTHESIS LECTURES ON INFORMATION CONCEPTS, RETRIEVAL, AND SERVICES #65

ABSTRACT

Information Retrieval performance measures are usually retrospective in nature, representing the effectiveness of an experimental process. However, in the sciences, phenomena may be predicted, given parameter values of the system. After developing a measure that can be applied retrospectively or can be predicted, performance of a system using a single term can be predicted given several different types of probabilistic distributions. Information Retrieval performance can be predicted with multiple terms, where statistical dependence between terms exists and is understood. These predictive models may be applied to realistic problems, and then the results may be used to validate the accuracy of the methods used. The application of metadata or index labels can be used to determine whether or not these features should be used in particular cases. Linguistic information, such as part-of-speech tag information, can increase the discrimination value of existing terminology and can be studied predictively.

This work provides methods for measuring performance that may be used predictively. Means of predicting these performance measures are provided, both for the simple case of a single term in the query and for multiple terms. Methods of applying these formulae are also suggested.

KEYWORDS

Information Retrieval, performance measures, science, predicting performance, single term models, statistical feature dependence, multiple features, metadata performance, natural language performance measures

Contents

Preface

In this book, we present both Information Retrieval performance measures and specific ways to compute and predict the values of the measures. While many different ways to evaluate performance have been suggested by scholars, only a few may be computed predictively based on characteristics of the data and the systems without going through the retrieval process itself. By focusing on predictable measures, a science of Information Retrieval performance can be developed where one can fully determine the value for certain performance measures, given certain other system characteristics. Knowing that an object will be traveling at twice a given velocity for an hour, one *knows* that the object will travel twice the distance. Such a widely understood relationship exists within physics, but little has been done to develop this kind of relationship in Information Retrieval. We suggest here that by choosing a predictable measure and then developing predictive formulae that relate other parameters of the data and the chosen performance variable, we may easily predict the performance and take advantage of these predictive rules in adding to the science of Information Retrieval.

How to validate these predictions of performance is discussed and the validation of these measures shown. While several million validating calculations have been successful at accurately predicting the empirical Information Retrieval performance, one could continue to conduct further validations to determine whether other circumstances might yield a failure in the accuracy of the predictive methods. The major limitation of this work is that it has only been tested on a relatively small number of data values, compared to the infinite number of possibilities that could be tested. While these millions of comparisons have shown consistently the perfect accuracy of these predictive formulae, the empirical results are consistent with the desired results in all cases examined that included one or two documents up to a dozen documents or so. If there were a size-related phenomenon, where the principles underlying the formula do not work the same once the number of documents reaches the hundreds or the hundreds of thousands, this scale-related phenomenon would not have been identified with the validation techniques used.

Basics of probability and a probabilistic model of Information Retrieval are provided in this work, to be used as the basis for other models discussed. After examining a range of performance measures, this work will focus on the Average Search Length (ASL), or, in a predictive mode, the Expected Position of a Relevant Document (EPRD). How to predict the EPRD in a system using only a single binary term will be examined. Other distributions for a single term will be considered, such as a Poisson distributed term and a normally distributed feature. Information Retrieval performance with multiple terms with dependencies are also examined and validated. Examples of how to use this form of performance prediction will be used to study the addition of metadata terms to a document, as well as part-of-speech tags added to terms.

Robert M. Losee
January 2019

Acknowledgments

When I spoke with Gary Marchionini about an idea I had for an extended article, he pointed out that this series might be a good place for such a paper. This work would not exist without Gary's proactive attitude and his support.

I would like to thank Norbert Fuhr for comments on an earlier draft of this work.

Lewis Church discussed the ideas behind predicting Information Retrieval performance over the course of several years, and his intellectual interest in the area provided an incentive to continue these studies. His comments on an earlier draft of this work were very valuable.

Caitlyn Kon provided useful comments on style and mathematical approaches.

Lee Ann Roush has discussed much of this work with the author and she, without hesitation, always provides useful and thoughtful comments.

All errors remain the responsibility of the author.

Robert M. Losee
January 2019

CHAPTER 1

Information Retrieval: A Predictive Science

Information Retrieval is the discipline that studies how recorded information is retrieved, as well as organized for use, and how the use and related needs develop and serve to drive the design and implementation of Information Retrieval systems. Studying how a document is retrieved, as well as the quality of the Information Retrieval process, can be performed using several different methods. One simple method is to perform experiments, trying different techniques—including different algorithms—with a given dataset, looking for performance improvements in the Information Retrieval processes. The TREC (Text REtrieval Conference) studies developed by the National Institute of Standards and Technology of the U.S. government provide datasets incorporating documents and queries that are used in the study of Information Retrieval performance, ideally allowing generalization to similar datasets, users, and domains. Psychology and sociology have developed techniques in survey design, interviewing, focus groups, and other techniques that can be applied to the social scientific study of searchers and contributors to Information Retrieval databases. Computer science has developed a range of research methods, such as those used in software engineering, to analyze the various aspects of algorithms, software modules, and development techniques. These methods can help place variables into their context as foundations upon which future evaluation may be conducted. Other non-TREC experimental studies often advance Information Retrieval, either for academic knowledge or for corporate advantage. Google, Microsoft, and Facebook, for example, conduct many "A/B" experiments, where almost all of their many machines continue to use the default algorithms that the company has developed, while a few machines use a variant of the algorithm to see how performance might improve with this variant. Because large technology companies function with so many users, one can determine the effectiveness of new techniques within brief time periods.

Developing scientific methods for Information Retrieval may provide regularities upon which both academic and commercial organizations may build improved Information Retrieval systems. A science of Information Retrieval or any other discipline usually begins by describing the phenomena in which it is interested. By observing large amounts of data, one can then describe accurately what is happening.

The relationships between variables may also be studied with mathematical arguments and proofs. When these analytic methods produce statements, we may assume that the statements are accurate if the argument is itself correct. While one may believe that one's argument is correct, verification through testing may also be conducted. The role of verification is debated, but both proofs and verification can serve to argue for specific relationships existing between variables. Proofs may be made using arguments that appear to be sound, containing no weaknesses or flaws. While most proofs are made using logic, mathematical, and human argumentation, advances in the ability of computer languages to produce proofs have resulted in computer-generated proofs that are considered to be of the same quality and nature as traditional human-produced proofs.

In cases where a proof is unavailable, the rules may be *validated* by trying them in a large number of cases, or, in some instances, in all possible cases. For example, it was noted in the 1800s that maps needed only four colors if they were to be drawn so that no two adjacent countries had the same color. While no mathematical proof of this was available, people continued to try to develop proofs. While not a formal mathematical proof, Kenneth Appel and Wolfgang Haken (1976, see Fritsch and Fritsch [1998]) were able to reduce the problem to showing that when each of 1,936 possible configurations met certain requirements, then four colors were sufficient for any map and that these configurations met these requirements. Further attempts at proofs were made, and improvements from the initial work of Appel and Haken further simplified the problem. Yet, many mathematicians continue to doubt that a large number of iterations through many problems show that the problem and suggested answer have been *proved* to be true. We present validations for some of the work below, suggesting that for large ranges of iterations, the rules developed hold. While we accept that these are not adequate as complete proofs, they do show that the results hold for a large, specified range of values. We expect that if rules are accurate for all databases of two to fourteen documents, then the rules likely will hold for all databases of documents.

Regressions provide a statistical technique that can predict values given the nature of the relationships among characteristics. A particular regression learns the relationship between one or more independent variables and predicts the value of the dependent variable—the outcome variable. A simple linear regression learns from one independent variable how to predict the dependent variable, while a multiple linear regression learns from more than one statistically independent variable how to predict the dependent variable, or outcome. In many realistic situations, the regression's multiple independent variables are not fully independent, yet predictions consistent with this independence assumption often provide results that may not be exactly correct but are good approximations of the correct result. Many simple regressions assume that the variables are normally distributed variables. However, many variables are not normally distributed, and these may be included in regressions by taking logarithmic transformations of the variables or relationships between these non-normal variables. Formulas in the next chapter are consistent with regressions using these logarithmic transformations.

1.1 RULES, MEASURES, AND SCIENCE

We are all familiar with many scientific rules. Physics provides the rule

$$distance = rate \times time \tag{1.1}$$

that is widely known and accepted. It can be used to predict how far we will travel in a certain amount of time or how long it will take to make a trip. Driving a car for 60 miles, or kilometers, per hour for 3 hours will take one 180 miles, or kilometers, respectively, a relationship understood by most adults. The accuracy of the relationship assumes that one drives a steady speed, while most actual drivers and vehicles vary their speed to some extent. There may be slight differences between individual vehicles. Driving on a road with no other cars may result in different behaviors than one might encounter driving on a congested road.

Note that this basic rule combining rate and time to yield distance requires time and rate to be accurate measures to compute distance accurately. We would not have simple consistently accurate rules if instead of distance measured using feet or meters or miles, we choose to measure distance subjectively as how far an individual runs in 10 s, or how far a child can throw a ball on his or her tenth birthday. These measures will vary between individuals and would stop the development of general rules, such as Equation (1.1).

The choice of variables is critical to the development of a science. The basic rules in physics have been derived, and given increased accuracy, due to advances over centuries in the development of measurement technology. The applications of physics have continued to increase in accuracy as the technology improves. Some of the common measures used in Information Retrieval have been more subjective and do not fit as well with scientific laws. The nature of some better, more predictable variables are discussed below.

1.2 THE SCIENCE OF INFORMATION RETRIEVAL

A science of Information Retrieval may be based upon a measure of expected positions for relevant documents in an ordered or partially ordered list of documents. Unlike most other measures used in traditional Information Retrieval studies, this average or expected value may be predictable. Most existing Information Retrieval performance measures do not need to be predictable, and have characteristics that make them unpredictable. For example, some measures ignore the position of non-relevant documents, making the value of the measures difficult to predict into the future. These hard-to-predict measures are still very useful in retrospective studies of retrieval performance, where one can arbitrarily develop techniques that allow them, for example, to skip the positions or precision values associated with non-relevant documents.

Most Information Retrieval studies attempt to show how a measure can be maximized by using a specific technique, given a certain dataset. Studying these techniques is valuable and can lead to an understanding of what combinations of techniques will result in the best obtainable performance.

Our goal here is different. Focusing more on how to predict Information Retrieval system performance, the research below develops both the measures that can be predicted and some rules that can be used to predict performance. The following options will be examined in developing this scientific approach to Information Retrieval:

1. a predictable, single number measure of retrieval performance;

2. a predictive model for single term systems;

3. a predictive model for multiple term systems; and

4. applications of these predictive techniques.

These measures address the ordering of relevant and non-relevant documents. Predicting Information Retrieval performance takes many of the variables available and is able to provide the desired performance measure without actual document ordering occurring.

CHAPTER 2

Probabilities and Probabilistic Information Retrieval

2.1 PROBABILITIES

Mathematical models can use any of a number of the various mathematical disciplines to describe a problem and to propose possible solutions. Algebraic, combinatoric, geometric, and probabilistic methods may be used to solve problems such as those presented in Information Retrieval applications. While the focus below is on probabilistic methods, other methods are certainly as valid and useful [Church, 2010]. The emphasis here on probabilistic methods is because of its history of developing predictive models in sciences. The probabilistic methods are applied to produce decision-based expressions of how systems should operate.

Random Variables   Variables in a mathematical description may take on a member of a set of attributes. Each of these variables may be referred to as a *random variable* when the attributes in the set of attributes may be described probabilistically. If we have a single fair die, with one to six dots on the six surfaces of the die, we may describe the chance of obtaining a surface with one dot on it as 1/6. Viewing the die as a random variable X may capture this, with the chance of one of the six values computed as

$$\Pr(X = x), \tag{2.1}$$

the probability that random variable X has the particular value x. If we are interested in whether the die takes on a particular value, for example, $x = 3$, we may denote this probability as

$$\Pr(X = 3) = \frac{1}{6}, \tag{2.2}$$

where the uppercase X denotes the random variable and 3 is the particular value, and where the case of the variable indicates that something is the random variable or the value of the variable. When we have $\Pr(X = 3)$ this may denote the probability that the random variable X takes on the value 3, whereas $\Pr(X = 6)$ would be the probability that a 6 would be obtained with the roll of the die.

The probability of a specific event with a single variable occurring is a *marginal probability*. Using Table 2.1, we can determine that the probability someone is an A is $(1 + 4)/10 = 0.5$ while the probability of being a B is computed as $(1 + 2)/10 = 0.3$.

Table 2.1: Sample data table

	A	Not A	Margin
B	1	2	(1 + 2)/10
Not B	4	3	(4 + 3)/10
Margin	(1 + 4)/10	(2 + 3)/10	10

Joint Probability   The probability of two events occurring together is referred to as the *joint probability*. The chance of being an A and a $\text{Not} B$ is the A column in Table 2.1 combined with the $\text{Not} B$ row; this intersection is 4/10. This would be denoted as $\Pr(A, \text{NotB}) = 4/10 = 0.4$. Using a comma in a probability implies the use of the joint probability.

Conditional Probability   A *conditional probability* is the chance that one feature has a certain value, given or assuming the presence of another variable. For example, one might ask what is the chance that one has brown hair, given that one is left-handed, or the chance that one has black hair, given that one is right-handed. Both of these assume a certain hand preference, and calculate the desired probability, given this preference or limiting oneself to the people with this handedness.

One can compute the probability that one is an A, given that one is a B, denoted as $\Pr(A|B)$, meaning that one is limiting oneself to the first row of Table 2.1. Given that limitation, where there are 3 cases that are B, the A case is one of the 3 cases in the first row, thus the conditional probability is $\Pr(A|B) = 1/3$.

2.2   PROBABILISTIC RETRIEVAL

Probabilistically justified decisions rules for document retrieval begin with retrieving a document if the expected cost of doing so is lower than the expected cost of not doing so [Bookstein, 1983]. By considering the document with feature d, one can estimate costs for retrieving a document and the cost for not retrieving a document given feature d or the absence of this value for the feature, $\overline{d}$. We assume that the expected cost of retrieving a document with feature set d is denoted as $EC(\text{ret}|d)$. Here

$$EC(\text{ret}|d) < EC(\overline{\text{ret}}|d), \tag{2.3}$$

the expected cost of retrieving a document with characteristic d is less than the expected cost of not retrieving a document with characteristic d, where a "cost" is a negative for any searcher.

One can expand the rule using the expected costs (Equation (2.3)) to suggest the following rule:

$$\Pr(\text{rel}|d)C_{\text{ret,rel}} + \Pr(\overline{\text{rel}}|d)C_{\text{ret},\overline{\text{rel}}} < \Pr(\text{rel}|d)C_{\overline{\text{ret}},\text{rel}} + \Pr(\overline{\text{rel}}, d)C_{\overline{\text{ret}},\overline{\text{rel}}}. \tag{2.4}$$

This may be algebraically manipulated to suggest that the following decision rule be used:

$$\frac{\Pr(\mathrm{rel}|d)}{\Pr(\overline{\mathrm{rel}}|d)} < C_{\mathrm{constant}}, \tag{2.5}$$

where the C_{constant} represents a constant combining the four different C cost values seen in Equation (2.4).

While this decision rule can be applied directly to each document, most Information Retrieval systems take the document weight, the left side of Equation (2.5), to be used to sort the documents (by this value), presenting the document most likely to be useful first, the second-best second on an ordered list of documents, and so on. [Robertson and Sparck Jones, 1976]. Obviously if one wants a binary "retrieve or not-retrieve" decision, such as whether to filter electronic email into an inbox or into a *Junk* email folder, one can use the rule as originally defined in Equation (2.4) and not sort the documents.

2.2.1 BAYES RULE

One can manipulate probabilities using Bayes rule, a principle that is useful for statistical manipulation. One begins with any joint probability being composed of the conditional probability of one feature given the other, multiplied by the probability of the other feature (as in the right-hand side of this): $\Pr(x, y) = \Pr(x|y)\Pr(y)$. Here, the probability of two variables together equals the probability of one variable given the other combined with the probability of the other.

By beginning with the two equivalent joint probabilities and then rewriting the two joint probabilities two different ways, and then dividing both sides by $\Pr(d)$, one obtains the following:

$$
\begin{aligned}
\Pr(h, d) &= \Pr(d, h) \\
\Pr(h|d)\Pr(d) &= \Pr(d|h)\Pr(h) \\
\Pr(h|d) &= \frac{\Pr(d|h)\Pr(h)}{\Pr(d)}.
\end{aligned}
\tag{2.6}
$$

We may understand the h above in Equation (2.6) as a hypothesis and d as some data. We can begin the last formula as $\Pr(h)$ on the right side, an *a priori* value; by combining this hypothesis $\Pr(h)$ with the likelihood data $\Pr(d|h)$ being included on the right-hand side of the equation, the $\Pr(h|d)$ provides the posterior hypothesis, on the left, given the data included on the right.

The odds for these values may be used:

$$\frac{\Pr(h|d)}{\Pr(\overline{h}|d)} = \frac{\Pr(d|h)\Pr(h)\Pr(d)}{\Pr(d|\overline{h})\Pr(\overline{h})\Pr(d)}. \tag{2.7}$$

We note that the $\Pr(d)$ component exists in both the numerator and denominator and cancels itself out. If we are using these odds to rank documents, the component $\Pr(h)/\Pr(\overline{h})$ is constant for all documents and can be dropped from consideration, simplifying the ranking process.

In the science of Information Retrieval, one often has the hypothesis that a document is relevant. One might then try to retrieve documents where

$$\frac{\Pr(d|\mathrm{rel})}{\Pr(d|\overline{\mathrm{rel}})} \tag{2.8}$$

is greater than a cost constant. One can also choose to rank documents by the value of $\Pr(d|\mathrm{rel})/\Pr(d|\overline{\mathrm{rel}})$. This may be referred to as the discrimination value of the feature: how well it separates the relevant from the non-relevant documents.

Example 2.1   Ordering Sample Documents. Assume that we have eight documents. Consider four documents with a query feature, with three of these documents relevant. There is one relevant document without the feature and three non-relevant documents without the feature. Thus, there are four relevant documents and four non-relevant documents. This produces

		Feature Present		
		N	Y	
Relevance	N	3	1	4
	Y	1	3	4
		4	4	

In this case, $\Pr(d|\mathrm{rel}) = 3/4$ and $\Pr(d|\overline{\mathrm{rel}}) = 1/4$. If a document has the feature, the value of our expression using Equation (2.8) is $(3/4)/(1/4)$. As a positive value, this indicates that this feature is a positive discriminator, that is, the feature is more likely to occur in a relevant than in a non-relevant document. A feature with a negative discrimination value would be an indicator that the feature is a better indicator of non-relevance than it is of relevance.

Log Odds and Additive Information   One can take the logarithm of both sides of Equation (2.7), after simplifying by canceling out the two $\Pr(d)$ components:

$$\log \frac{\Pr(h|d)}{\Pr(\overline{h}|d)} = \log \frac{\Pr(d|h)\Pr(h)}{\Pr(d|\overline{h})\Pr(\overline{h})}. \tag{2.9}$$

Since $\Pr(h)/\Pr(\overline{h})$ is constant, if we wish to rank documents, this component may be dropped, producing

$$= \log \frac{\Pr(d|h)}{\Pr(d|\overline{h})}. \tag{2.10}$$

Example 2.2   Log-odds. Using logarithms to base 2, the data in the previous example, where the log odds of $\log_2((3/4)/(1/4)) = 1.584$ bits, suggests that there is a positive amount of data supporting that this feature is a positive discriminator. If the number of bits from Equation (2.10) is a negative value, this suggests that the feature is a negative discriminator, and that the presence of the feature in a documents argues that the document is likely a non-relevant document.

2.3   DESCRIBING A PROBABILITY

Conjugate prior distributions represent probabilities that can represent whatever knowledge we have about a particular probability. They can represent ignorance or a high degree of knowledge about a particular probability. The conjugate nature of a distribution is such that the knowledge we have about a p value is incorporated into the parameters of a beta distribution. Similarly, the λ value for the Poisson distributed terms, such as term frequency data, uses the gamma distribution to represent the prior knowledge about the λ components, as well as the degree of knowledge about the parameter.

Example 2.3   Incomplete Beta Distribution. The Incomplete beta distribution represents the knowledge about the p component in a binary distribution.

$$\beta_x^y(a,b) = \frac{\Gamma(a+b)}{\Gamma(a)\Gamma(b)} \int_x^y p^{a-1}(1-p)^{b-1} dp. \tag{2.11}$$

In Information Retrieval applications, the parameters a and b can be used to represent the number of relevant documents retrieved and the number of documents retrieved. As the number of documents retrieved increases, the variance decreases, representing increased confidence in our knowledge about the value of p. Figure 2.1 shows three beta distributions; as more knowledge is gained about the value of p, the Beta distribution shows a lower and lower variance and has a higher peak.

The Beta distribution can be parameterized in different ways. If we consider the case where we have a coin that can only land as heads or tails when tossed, then knowing two of the three factors—the number of coins tossed, the number of heads obtained, and the number of tails obtained—will always allow us to determine the value of the third parameter. The Beta distribution may be parameterized to use any two of these, with the third value being something one can easily compute arithmetically. Thus, when reading literature in this area, one will see different forms of the Beta distribution, different means and estimates of p, as well as other parameterizations. The Beta distribution represented by the horizontal line in Figure 2.1 represents the Beta distribution with parameters 1, 1 and shows a non-informative distribution, where we have no confidence whatsoever about the actual value of p.

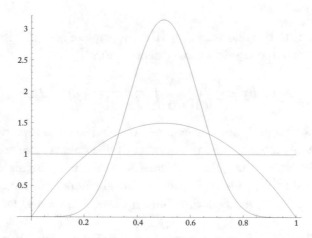

Figure 2.1: Three different Beta distributions with parameters, moving from non-informative (the straight line across the graph) to parameters 4,4, which produce the most peaked Beta distribution. The more data that is included, the more peaked the distribution becomes, generally representing more confidence (less variance) for the parameters p.

CHAPTER 3

Information Retrieval Performance Measures

How does one evaluate a system's performance, given that some values are considered desirable and some other values may best be avoided? Many Information Retrieval system measures emphasize the placement of *relevant* documents early in an ordered list of documents. These relevant documents may be viewed as being judged to be on the topic of interest expressed in the query, or the documents may be useful or novel to the user. Relevance also may be understood as being useful to address the needs expressed in a query, as being accessible, or many other possible variants. Topical relevance is commonly used in Information Retrieval experimentation on computers.

The use of these performance measures can serve to both study the ordering supplied by a retrieval system, as well as the assignment of index terms through automatic indexing systems [Manning et al., 2008]. Referred to as the Cranfield model of performance studies [Cleverdon, 1967], these measures can be applied to the assignment of terms in relevant and non-relevant documents, as well as the ordering of documents by a retrieval system.

3.1 PRECISION AND RECALL

Although many measures have been used to evaluate retrieval systems, precision and recall are some of the earliest measures and have served as the basis for probably more studies than any other measures.

3.1.1 PRECISION

The precision measure,

$$\text{Precision} = \frac{R_{\text{ret}}}{R_{ret} + N_{ret}}, \tag{3.1}$$

uses R_{ret} as the number of relevant documents that have been retrieved, and $R_{ret} + N_{ret}$ represents the number of retrieved documents from the database.

Informally, precision may be understood as the quality of the retrieved documents. If one had 4 documents retrieved, and 2 of them were relevant, then the precision would be .50. The best possible situation with 4 retrieved documents would be that all 4 are relevant, and precision would thus be 1.00, that is, 100% of the documents retrieved.

A probabilistic measure or estimate of precision P is

$$\text{Precision} = \Pr(\text{rel}|\text{ret}) \tag{3.2}$$

and this may be useful when estimating many of the values and techniques below.

3.1.2   RECALL

The recall measure is computed as:

$$\text{Recall} = \frac{R_{\text{ret}}}{R}, \tag{3.3}$$

where R_{ret} is the number of documents that have been retrieved and are relevant and R represents the number of relevant documents in the database.

Informally, recall may be understood as the progress on the journey to retrieve all the relevant documents. If there were 4 relevant documents in the database and 2 of the 4 documents retrieved were relevant, then the recall would be .50, that is, half of the relevant documents have been retrieved. If there were 3 relevant documents from among 10 documents retrieved with the database having 4 relevant documents, the recall would be 0.75. Note that we could compute the precision for the latter scenario, because 3/10 of the retrieved documents are relevant.

A probabilistic measure or estimate of recall is

$$\text{Recall} = \Pr(\text{ret}|\text{rel}). \tag{3.4}$$

3.2   PRECISION-RECALL GRAPHS

We can graph precision and recall together, with precision always being a value on the y axis and recall always being a value on the x axis.

Example 3.1   Consider the following documents, with the subscripts indicating relevance ("r") or non-relevance ("n"):

$$d_r, d_r, d_n, d_r, d_n, d_r, d_n, d_n, d_r, d_n, d_n, d_r.$$

The precision may be computed over the entire list of values, taken from left to right, as the precision list: 1.00, 1.00, 0.67, 0.75, 0.60, 0.67, 0.57, 0.50, 0.56, 0.50, 0.45, 0.50 and the recall is: 0.17, 0.33, 0.33, 0.50, 0.50, 0.67, 0.67, 0.67, 0.83, 0.83, 0.83, 1.00. For the first data point, which is a relevant document, one has retrieved a single document, which is relevant. Thus, the precision is 1.00, because 100% of the retrieved documents (one document) are relevant. The recall after this first document retrieved is 17% because 1 of the 6 relevant documents has been retrieved. When evaluating basic plots with an x and a y axis, there is normally a single y value for each x value. Thus, these multiple precision values for a single recall value are not acceptable.

We can then arrive at Figure 3.1, which shows how there may be multiple precision values for many recall points. However, one may want only one precision point for each of the recall

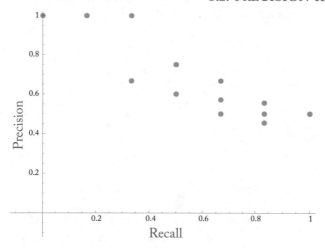

Figure 3.1: Multiple precision values for several recall levels.

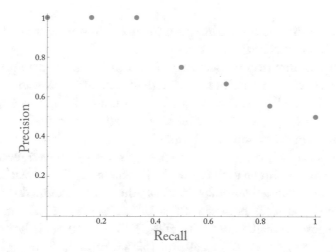

Figure 3.2: Using only one precision per recall level.

points. This is usually accomplished by selecting the highest precision point for each recall point, and this is the highest point in Figure 3.1, exaggerating the precision value.

Figure 3.2 shows the set of points with only these highest values included. While this can be included, the data in Figure 3.2 does not have connected points. If one wishes to connect these precision recall points, one can use a straight line, such as in Figure 3.3. Raghavan et al. [1989] discuss using the ceiling or best measure for precision values and provides an interpolation

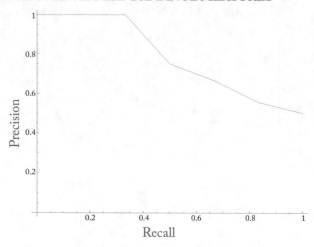

Figure 3.3: Precision-Recall graph with points connected.

technique that better addresses comparing performance values when not all of the documents with a particular set of characteristics are retrieved.

Connecting the points may be necessary if one wishes to average precision values over large numbers of queries. Many queries have different numbers of relevant documents, and the fractional values for the recall points will vary. If there were 4 relevant documents, there will be 4 recall values, of 1/4, 2/4, 3/4, and 4/4. If there was another query with 5 relevant documents, then there will be different recall values, including 1/5, 2/5, 3/5, 4/5, and 5/5. Determining the average precision values may involve taking the precision values at given recall points, or it may take a precision value for a point on each one of the interpolating lines. Recall is often computed for some values that are rounded numbers. Some studies have examined the average precision values computed for decile recall points, such as 10%, 20%, 30% recall, and so forth. Others have examined precision at recall points 25%, 50%, 75%, and 100%. It is usually assumed that the starting point for each line is at 0% recall and 100% precision, the upper-left corner of each precision-recall graph.

3.2.1 HIGH-PRECISION SYSTEMS AND HIGH-RECALL SYSTEMS

Precision-Recall graphs generally move from the upper-left corner of the graph to the lower-right portion of the graph. A given Information Retrieval system may be developed to emphasize retrieval over the full range of recall values, depending on the system parameters. *High-recall* is where the system is designed to retrieve most relevant documents so that high-recall is normally achieved for a given query. Some users, such as academics and lawyers, may explicitly wish to find everything on a topic. A medical researcher may seek all references to a particular drug or to a disease. Patent lawyers may need to find every invention that has certain characteristics. University students and faculty and researchers often need to examine all the material in a particular research area. Measures, such as recall and precision-recall curves, are very useful when studying high-recall systems.

High-precision systems, on the other hand, aim for strong performance on the left-hand side of a precision-recall curve. Someone seeking one fact or a single web page might be satisfied with one or two web pages that directly address the information need. Most Internet searches with a cellular telephone with computational capabilities (a "smart phone") are not trying to find a comprehensive set of documents but instead seek a small number of documents or answers to a need. As more and more searching focuses on a single answer that might be on one of the first few web pages retrieved, high-precision searching has become an increasingly larger proportion of the searches conducted on a given day.

While most research about searching in the early phases of Information Retrieval emphasized high-recall, retrieval has more recently shifted to also address high-precision searching. Much of the discussion below will emphasize high-recall searching, which might seem old-fashioned to some, with some discussion of how to apply these techniques to high-precision searching.

3.2.2   GENERALITY AND FALLOUT

In addition to precision and recall, two other measures, *fallout* and *generality*, are useful in similar situations. These four measures combine together, as will be seen shortly. Just as recall is the percent of relevant documents that have been retrieved, *fallout* is the percent of the non-relevant documents in the database that have been retrieved. Clearly, this complements recall. *Generality* is the percent of relevant documents in the database, a measure of density. Van Rijsbergen [1979] notes that, given Precision, Recall, F, and G for precision, recall, fallout, and generality, respectively, we may compute the relationship between the four variables as

$$\text{Precision} = \frac{\text{Recall} \times G}{(\text{Recall} \times G) + F \times (1 - G)}. \tag{3.5}$$

One may algebraically solve for any one variable from the other three variables.

3.3   HIGH-PRECISION PERFORMANCE MEASURES

3.3.1   MEAN AVERAGE PRECISION

The Mean Average Precision (MAP) represents the average of the precision values computed at the points where relevant documents occur. Note that ties are not explicitly addressed. Furthermore, while this is superficially similar to the Average Search Length (ASL) measure in some respects, MAP uses only those documents from among the first n documents. One can similarly use a normalized ASL measure for the first n documents.

Example 3.2   MAP Example. The MAP may be computed for the precision and recall values described earlier in this chapter:

$$MAP = (1 + 1 + .75 + .66 + .55 + .50)/6 = 7.44.$$

3.3.2   PRECISION AT k

The precision at k measure computes the precision only for the first k documents. The variable k is usually a small number, such as 10 or 25. This supports the concerns of those who desire high-precision and focuses on the first documents retrieved. It does not emphasize the ordering within the first k documents, like the discounted Cumulative Gain measure below.

3.3.3   DISCOUNTED CUMULATIVE GAIN

The Discounted Cumulative Gain (DCG) is a measure, like MAP, that emphasizes the first several documents. With the DCG computed as

$$DCG = \sum_{i=1}^{Pos} \frac{rel_i}{\log_2(i+1)}, \tag{3.6}$$

where Pos is the final position, and i iterates through all the positions up to Pos. The variable rel_i represents the relevance value at position i. Note that rel_i can be any value from 0 up, and thus the DCG measure is based on a non-binary weighting of individual documents, unlike most of the other performance measures discussed here. The more relevant the documents retrieved earlier in the retrieval process, the higher the DCG.

3.3.4   F MEASURE

The combination of precision and recall has long been a goal of those evaluating retrieval systems. Computing the harmonic mean of precision and recall has been one popular solution. Computed as

$$F = \frac{2}{\frac{1}{Recall} + \frac{1}{Precision}}, \tag{3.7}$$

the F measure serves to combine both precision and recall.

When using F, a value is obtained for each specific recall and precision point. If F is to be used as a single number measure of retrieval performance, it is often computed as the optimal F: that pair of precision and recall values that produces the highest F value.

3.3.5   MEAN RECIPROCAL RANK

The Mean Reciprocal Rank (MRR) is measured over a set of queries. The inverse of the rank for the first occurrence of each query term is computed over each of the queries. Thus, if each query term is first in the list of retrieved document terms, the MRR is 1. If the first query term is at rank 1, the second at rank 2, and the third at rank 3, then the MRR is the average $(1/1 + 1/2 + 1/3)/3$. The reciprocal of the MRR is the harmonic mean of the ranks.

3.4   RECEIVER OPERATING CHARACTERISTIC

The *receiver operating characteristic* (ROC) curve shows the relationship between increasing the retrieval of relevant documents and increasing the number of documents as a whole. Figure 3.4 shows how as documents are retrieved, the proportion of relevant documents increases at a higher rate than random. The dashed line from the lower left to the upper right represents the trend where the proportion of relevant documents retrieved equals the proportion of all documents that are retrieved.

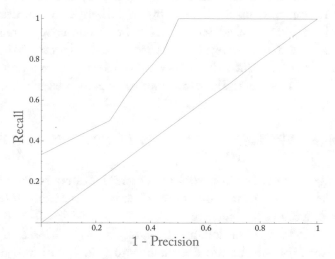

Figure 3.4: Receiver operating characteristic curve.

The ROC curve may be viewed more generally, describing signal and noise and how they can be separated. In any signal receiver, the signal and noise must be separated. A ROC figure shows how well the signal, on the y axis, exceeds and is separable from the noise on the x axis.

The distance between a line perpendicular to the diagonal line representing random performance and reaching to the ROC is proportional to the difference between the signal and the noise. As this distance increases, the *detection threshold* increases and the ability to retrieve information and signals increases.

3.5   SEARCH LENGTHS

Search length measures represent the number of documents examined by an end user. As the average number of documents retrieved, it can represent a unit of work that most people can easily understand.

3.5.1   EXPECTED SEARCH LENGTH

Cooper [1968] proposed the Expected Search Length (ESL) measure as an indicator of the amount of work used to retrieve the desired number of relevant documents. By counting only the non-relevant documents retrieved, ESL captures the cost of retrieving each of the non-relevant documents up to the position of the average position of a relevant document. This treats non-relevant documents as having a cost while relevant documents don't place a cost or burden on the searcher.

Example 3.3   Consider a set of documents, $(d_r, d_r, d_n, d_r, d_n, d_n, d_r)$, with relevant documents represented by d_r and non-relevant documents by a d_n. There are no non-relevant documents retrieved for either of the first two relevant documents, 1 non-relevant document retrieved for the third relevant document, and 3 non-relevant documents retrieved for the last relevant document. The average number of non-relevant documents retrieved for these 4 relevant documents is $(0 + 0 + 1 + 3)/4 = 4/4 = 1$ document. The total number of non-relevant documents is $0 + 0 + 1 + 3 = 4$ documents.

3.5.2   AVERAGE SEARCH LENGTH AND THE EXPECTED POSITION OF A RELEVANT DOCUMENT

The ASL is the average number of documents, either relevant or non-relevant, that are retrieved while searching the set of documents for relevant documents, the number of documents up to the average position of a relevant document.

If we had the following set of documents, d_r, d_r, d_n, d_r, retrieved in order from left to right, then the positions for the relevant documents are 1, 2, 4, with the average of the three positions for relevant documents as $(1 + 2 + 4)/3 = 7/3 = 2$ and $1/3$.

Ties and strong ordering vs. weak   Consider the following arrangement of documents, along with whether the document weights are tied or not for a given query:

$$\left| \; d_r \; \left| \; d_n \; \right| \; d_r \; \right| \; d_r \; \left| \; d_n \; \right| \; d_r \; \right|$$
$$\text{—Tie—}$$

We can compute that if we ignore the ties and take the documents directly as provided, the ASL is $(1 + 3 + 4 + 6)/4 = 14/4 = 3.50$. If ties are taken into consideration, we note that the second and the third documents have tied positional weights. The position for the second *and* the third documents is now the midpoint for the two, that is, position 2.5. Computing the ASL for this set of tied documents now places the second relevant document at position 2.5, so the ASL is now computed as $(1 + 2.5 + 4 + 6)/4 = 3.375$.

EPRD   The EPRD is the probabilistic and predictive version of the ASL. By using the probability of being at a particular position, one may predict into the future what the expected position (the prediction of the future average) is of a relevant document among the ordered documents. This will be examined in more detail in the next chapter. We now have the ASL or EPRD, which can serve as a useful single number measure of retrieval performance that is retrospective or predictive, respectively.

A scaled measure of ASL or EPRD performance, denoted as m, can be used to develop several other scaled measures. If we wish to develop a measure that analyzes this m value compared to the minimum m_{best} search length value, we can compute $m - m_{\text{best}}$. If we had 6 relevant documents, for example, the best possible ASL would be with all 6 documents at the front of the list, with the value $(1 + 2 + 3 + 4 + 5 + 6)/6 = 3.5$.

Best-Case ASL   In general, given R relevant documents, $m_{\text{best}} = (R + 1)/2$.

Worst-Case ASL   The worst case ASL or EPRD is denoted as $m_{\text{worst}} = N + (R + 1)/2$, given N non-relevant values.

The m value can now be scaled between its maximum and minimum value so that

$$m_{\text{scaled}} = \frac{|m_{\text{worst}} - m|}{m_{\text{worst}} - m_{\text{best}}},\tag{3.8}$$

where the numerator determines the difference between the measure m and its worst case, the largest possible m, normalized by dividing by the difference between the best and the worst case measures. If the performance is perfect and at its best possible value, then $m_{\text{scaled}} = 1$. If the performance is worst case, then $m_{\text{scaled}} = 0$.

Most "high precision" measures that examine the performance for the first several documents retrieved have an arbitrary cutoff for examining the documents, or have an arbitrarily chosen gradient favoring the earlier retrieved documents. Search length measures such as ASL may be similarly viewed as high-precision measures if one wishes to use them with an arbitrary cutoff.

PowerRank   The PowerRank measure proposed by Meng (Meng and Clark [2005] and Meng [2006]) begins with the ASL (or EPRD) and then divides it by the number of relevant documents retrieved. This functions as a high-precision measure, emphasizing the earlier retrieval of relevant documents. Below we emphasize the prediction of EPRD, but we can modify its estimate in most cases by dividing it by the number of relevant documents retrieved, producing an estimate supportive of addressing high-precision concerns.

3.6   SUMMARY

Most measures of Information Retrieval performance are designed to be used retrospectively. We consider these measures, as well as a predictive search length measures the EPRD. Precision and recall are two of the most frequently used measures, with precision being the quality of a retrieved set of documents, and recall being the proportion of relevant documents that are retrieved. Several measures that are high-precision measures are examined, including MAP and DCG measures. The ROC curve is used in a range of areas, many beyond Information Retrieval, to evaluate the difference between the performance and random performance. Search lengths are also considered, both ESL and ASL, and means for predicting a search length measure are discussed.

CHAPTER 4

Single-Term Performance

In the preceding chapter, we discussed several measures of performance, including the single-number performance measure ASL. Here we examine how ASL may be predicted as the EPRD. Below we develop a simple method of predicting this measure in the case of a single term. The simplest model of Information Retrieval performance is consistent with a single term assumption, where each query and each document is viewed as having or not having a particular, single (binary) term. When we have completed Chapter 4, we will examine more complex models in Chapter 5 where multiple different terms in a query and in documents are considered, and in that chapter, we will examine term dependence and how term independence may be used in this model of Information Retrieval performance.

4.1   A SINGLE BINARY TERM

Let us assume that we have a single query term and that documents are arranged so that those with the term are placed ahead of those documents without the term. In this situation, the term is a positive relevance discriminator; informally, the term is a good query term and using this term results in a greater rate of relevant documents than non-relevant documents being retrieved. More formally, a positive discriminator occurs with greater probability in relevant documents than in non-relevant documents. Using the parameters frequently used in describing probabilistic retrieval models, we may define the percent of relevant documents that contain the term as $p = \Pr(d|\text{rel})$. The percent of all documents that contain the term is denoted as $t = \Pr(d|\text{all}) = \Pr(d)$.

The EPRD in this ordered set of documents is composed of the EPRD in documents with the feature and the EPRD in documents without the feature.

We can compute the scaled EPRDs A, as:

$$A = \Pr(d|rel)\Pr(d)/2 + \Pr(\overline{d}|\text{rel})(1 - \Pr(\overline{d})/2). \qquad (4.1)$$

The $\Pr(d)$ component, dividing by 2, finds the center of the location where the terms occur, while the $\Pr(d|rel)$ component addresses the probability that the term occurs. As the position multiplied by the probability of being in this position for both documents with the term and documents without the term, this formula for A addresses both the feature or term being present (d) or absent $(\overline{d})$, both of the situations that occur with a single binary feature. The EPRD in the middle of the documents with the feature is the estimated middle of the position of documents with the feature, while the EPRD among the documents without the feature is the estimated middle of the documents without the feature. Since the documents are ordered so that those with the feature are ordered ahead of those documents without the feature, assuming the query feature is a positive discriminator, the EPRD in all the documents will be a weighted sum of the EPRDs in those documents with the feature, and the EPRDs in those documents without the feature as in Equation (4.1).

Equation (4.1) may be simplified using algebra to

$$A = \frac{1 + \Pr(d) - \Pr(d \,|\mathrm{rel})}{2}. \tag{4.2}$$

Given that $p = \Pr(d \,|\mathrm{rel})$ and $t = \Pr(d)$, this leads us to

$$A = \frac{1 - p + t}{2}. \tag{4.3}$$

Non-probabilistic models of these mean positions of relevant documents may be used. Lewis Church [2010] has done extensive development of models that can predict retrieval performance using combinatoric models. By emphasizing enumeration of structures, one can develop performance predictors similar to what was proposed above but without using probabilistic methods.

Example 4.1   Consider the case where there are 10 documents, 5 of them with the term in the query. Assume that there are 5 relevant documents, all of them with the query term. We assume that the documents are ordered rationally, so that those with the term are ahead of those without the term, and that the probability of optimal ordering $Q = 1$. In this case, the probability of having the term in question is $p = 5/5 = 1.0$. Similarly, the unconditional probability of any document having the term in question is $t = 5/10 = 0.5$. In this case, $A = (1 - 1.0 + 0.5)/2 = 0.25$. This value for A will be used below as the scaled EPRD.

Example 4.2   Best Case for A. The best-case performance occurs when A approaches 0. Consider a case when $p = 1$ and $t = 0.0001$, with t not being 0 since probabilities cannot be 0 (the probability that a document has the term in question close to 0) because the high $\Pr(d_i \,|\mathrm{rel}) = p$ value shows that, among the relevant documents, most have the term in question, moving the value of t away from 0. In this case, $A = (1 - 1 + 0.0001)/2 = 0.00005$.

Example 4.3   Worst Case for A. Similarly, we can consider the case where the A value approaches its worst-case performance. Consider where $\Pr(d_i \,|\mathrm{all}) = t = 0.999$, that is, almost all documents have the query term, and $\Pr(d_i \,|\mathrm{rel}) = p = 0.0001$, and among the relevant documents, almost none have the term in question. In this case, $A = (1 - 0.0001 + 0.999)/2 = 0.99945$, a very high value, reflecting a low level of performance.

Example 4.4   Random Performance. Random performance can exist when the term in the query doesn't seem to discriminate either positively or negatively. Consider when half the documents have the query term and half the relevant documents have the query term. In this case,

$Pr(d_i|rel) = p = 0.5$ and $Pr(d_i|all) = t = 0.5$. Thus, $A = (1 - 0.5 + 0.5)/2 = 1/2$. Generally, while $p = t$ then $A = 1/2$.

4.2   AVERAGE SEARCH LENGTH AND EXPECTED POSITION OF A RELEVANT DOCUMENT

Moving to a situation with $\mathcal{N}$ documents and assuming optimal ranking, the EPRD may be computed as:

$$\text{EPRD} = \mathcal{N}A + \frac{1}{2} = \mathcal{N}\left(\frac{1 - p + t}{2}\right) + \frac{1}{2}. \qquad (4.4)$$

Example 4.5   Predicting EPRD. We have a set of relevant and non-relevant documents, $d_{r,1}, d_{r,1}, d_{r,0}, d_{n,1}, d_{n,0}, d_{n,0}$, where the second subscript indicates the frequency of d in the document and r and n indicate whether the document is relevant or non-relevant to the query. The ordering would be such that documents with $d_{*,1}$, documents with the term, would be first, followed by documents with $d_{*,0}$, documents without the term. The ordering would thus be $d_{r,1}, d_{r,1}, d_{n,1}$ as a group, with the next documents being $d_{r,0}, d_{n,0}, d_{n,0}$. The parameters become $Pr(d_i|rel) = p = 2/3$ because of the three relevant documents, $d_{r,1}, d_{r,1}$, and $d_{r,0}$, with 2/3 of the relevant documents having the feature in question with a subscript of 1. For all the documents, with $d_{r,1}, d_{r,1}, d_{r,0}, d_{n,1}, d_{n,0}$, and $d_{n,0}$, 3 of the documents have the feature in question with a subscript of 1, and thus $Pr(d_i|all) = t = 3/6$. We also have $\mathcal{N} = 6$. Thus, $A = (1 - 2/3 + 3/6)/2 = 2.5/6$. The EPRD becomes $\text{EPRD} = \mathcal{N}A + 1/2 = 6((1 - (2/3) + (3/6))/2) + 1/2 = (6 * (2.5/6)) + 1/2 = 3$.

One could informally compute the ASL from the original data by noting that the first 2 relevant documents are tied for being at position 2, the middle position for the three documents with the feature of 1, and the last relevant document would be at position 5, with the average position being at $(2 + 2 + 5)/3 = 3$. The parametric formula for EPRD used in Equations (4.3) and (4.4) gives us the same result as computing the ASL through traditional methods.

Example 4.6   Predicting EPRD from Documents. Consider the following documents and relevance values that focus on the term *wind* (assumed to be the query term) for work on wind turbines:

Title	Relevance	Frequency of "Wind"
Wind in the Willows	N	1
Gone with the Wind	N	1
Wind Tunnels	N	1
Wind Power	Y	1
Wind Turbines	Y	1
The Cat in the Hat	N	0.

Given this data, one can compute the parameters $p = 2/2 = 1$ as both relevant documents have the feature *wind*, $t = 5/6$, as of all 6 documents, 5 of them have the feature, and $\mathcal{N} = 6$. One can compute $A = (1 - 1 + 5/6)/2 = 5/12$. Now one may compute EPRD $= \mathcal{N}A + 1/2 = 6(5/12) + 1/2 = 3$.

If we examine the documents themselves we note that the presence of the term *wind* is a positive discriminator. Ordering the 5 documents with the term ahead of the document without the term, we find that the average position for the two relevant documents is the center of the 5 documents, with the average position for positions 1, 2, 3, 4, and 5 being position 3, providing an informal argument for why the EPRD calculation in the previous paragraph produces the correct answer of $(3 + 3)/2 = 3$.

4.3   PROBABILITY OF OPTIMAL RANKING (Q)

Most Information Retrieval systems and search engines rank documents based on an algorithm. Those with better ranking formulas provide a better ranking in commercial situations and usually obtain more users. Systems usually attempt to provide the best ranking possible, but these systems are usually sub-optimal, but some of them will be optimal for a given search. When we have one binary feature, a rational ordering will keep documents with the feature together, and those documents without the feature will be kept together. When there is a single feature, and all documents with the feature are grouped together and all those without the feature are grouped together, then there will be 2^1 groups of documents, one group with the feature and one group with those documents without the feature. If there are two features there will be 2^2 groups of documents, 2^3 groups of documents with 3 features, and so forth. The simplest situation is with $2^1 = 2$ groups, and the probability of optimal ranking $Q = 1$ and $\overline{Q} = 0$.

The probability of optimal ranking, Q, is the probability that the ranking algorithm produces the best possible ranking. The value of Q will be 1 only when the algorithm produces an optimal ranking, no matter what data occurs which the algorithm uses in computing the ranking. Usually the algorithms are not perfect, such as when the author of a document about a particular pet animal uses the scientific name for the pet instead of the common name that the searcher used, making matching difficult. Assuming that $Q = 1$ is an approximation for most modern searches, but obviously a more accurate estimate of Q will result in a more accurate prediction of Information Retrieval performance.

Defining Q is clearly a probabilistic process, as the basic definition of Q is the probability that two rankings are the same. In simple cases, such as when there is a single, discrete feature, it may be practical to define Q using other methods, such as using combinatoric methods [Church, 2010]. Defining Q probabilistically may produce the simplest approach, and thus we follow this methodology below.

The probability of optimal ranking Q in the case of such a binary feature will typically be above one half, with the probability of the worst-case ranking being below one half. If this were not to be the case, then the ordering would be reversed so that the Q value will be above one half and the probability of the worst-case ranking will be below one half.

For much of our discussion, we will examine Q for binary features, where there are only two possible orderings. However, we might consider that when there are two features, there may be four different orderings, while with three different features there will be eight different orderings. It is much easier to examine the probability of optimal ordering with a single feature!

4.3.1   DEVELOPING Q

Let us assume that we have optimal ordering with a single term. This occurs when the term in question is a positive discriminator, that is, the term occurs at a higher rate in relevant documents than in all documents. If this is the case, the probability that a term occurs in relevant documents is greater than the probability that it occurs in an average document or all documents, and thus $p > t$.

The probability that optimal ranking occurs when ranking is provided by another ranking algorithm will be determined by the joint probability that optimal ranking occurs with that algorithm and the relationship $p > t$. The value for Q is usually written as the sum of two probabilities, the first being where features with 1 are ordered before features with 0, also denoted as $1 \succ 0$, and where the second probability represents the other ordering where documents with feature frequency of 0 are ordered before those with 1, denoted as $1 \preceq 0$.

4.3.2   BEST-CASE RANKING

In the best case, the Q value will be calculated as

$$Q = \Pr(p > t, p > t, 1 \succ 0) + \Pr(p \leq t, p \leq t, 1 \preceq 0) = 1, \qquad (4.5)$$

for all values of p and t, the joint probability that we have the given ranking method and optimal ranking. We find that Q is used for best-case ranking and $\overline{Q}$ for worst-case ranking, and $Q + \overline{Q} = 1$, when using a single feature.

4.3.3   INTERPRETING $\Pr(p > t)$

The probability that the variable p is greater than t is meant to address the degree of overlap between the optimal and the ranking algorithm in question. The variable p may have a range of values, and may be described by a probabilistic distribution, and the variable t may also be defined probabilistically. These two may overlap quite a bit, or they may be identical, or there may be no overlap at all between the probabilistic distributions describing p and t. If one views t as a point probability and p is a continuous distribution, then this becomes that portion of the p distribution that is above t or to the left of it, when graphed in a customary fashion. The combination of p and t determines the joint probability $\Pr(p > t)$.

4.3.4 WORST-CASE RANKING

In the worst case, the Q value will be calculated as

$$
\begin{aligned}
Q_{\text{Worst}} &= \Pr(p > t, p \leq t, 1 \succ 0) + \Pr(p \leq t, p > t, 1 \preceq 0) \\
&= \Pr(p > t, \neg(p > t), 1 \succ 0) + \Pr(p \leq t, \neg(p \leq t), 1 \preceq 0) \\
&= 0.
\end{aligned}
\tag{4.6}
$$

4.3.5 RANDOM RANKING

In the random case, the Q value will be calculated as

$$
Q = \Pr\left(p > t, \frac{p > t}{2}, 1 \succ 0\right) + \Pr\left(p \leq t, \frac{p \leq t}{2}, 1 \preceq 0\right).
\tag{4.7}
$$

The fractions, where we divide $\Pr(p > t)$ by 2 and $\Pr(p \leq t)$ by 2, splits the probabilities. We take only half the left-hand side (optimal ranking) and half the right-hand side (worst-case ranking), reducing this equation to something closer to $1/2$.

Below, other specific retrieval ranking algorithms are examined and their Q values determined. Note that we emphasize simple approaches to Q; more complex combinatoric models of Q are provided by Church [2010].

4.3.6 Q AND RANKING BY INVERSE DOCUMENT FREQUENCY WEIGHTING

The popular Inverse Document Frequency weighting has the following probability of optimal ranking:

$$
\begin{aligned}
Q_{\text{IDF}} &= \Pr(p > t, t > 0, 1 \succ 0) + \Pr(p \leq t, t \leq 0, 1 \preceq 0) \\
&= \Pr(p > t).
\end{aligned}
\tag{4.8}
$$

Church [2010] suggests improved procedures for computing the values for Q which better address boundary conditions.

Example 4.7   IDF Weighting and Q with the Text Titles example. Using the data in Example 4.6 on Page 23, we can see that in this one situation with 6 documents, $p = 1$ and $t = 5/6$, then $Q = 1$.

4.3.7 Q AND RANKING BY DECISION-THEORETIC WEIGHTING

Given Decision Theoretic weighting of terms and documents, the probability of optimal ranking provided by this weighting is:

$$
\log\left(\frac{p/(1-p)}{q/(1-q)}\right) > 0
$$

when $p > q$.

In other circumstances:

$$\log\left(\frac{p/(1-p)}{q/(1-q)}\right) \leq 0$$

when $p \leq q$.

$$Q_{\mathrm{DT}} = \Pr(p > t, p > q, 1 \succ 0) + \Pr(p \leq t, p \leq q, 1 \preceq 0). \tag{4.9}$$

An alternative version of this is to compute

$$Q_{\mathrm{DT}} = 1 - (\Pr(p > \max(t,q), 1 \succ 0) + \Pr(p \leq \min(t,q), 1 \preceq 0)). \tag{4.10}$$

4.4 EXPECTED POSITION OF A RELEVANT DOCUMENT GIVEN Q AND A VALUES

The EPRD may be computed assuming perfect ranking (or near perfect ranking) and thus without Q values, as was seen with Equation (4.4). However, computing the EPRD may take advantage of the Q value, by noting that we may weight the A and $\overline{A}$ values. Here the EPRD may be calculated as the weighting of A values for a single feature:

$$\mathrm{EPRD} = \mathcal{N}\left(AQ + \overline{A}\,\overline{Q}\right) + \frac{1}{2}. \tag{4.11}$$

We have two possible orderings, one with the feature being ordered first and the second with the feature being ordered last. One of these has the ordering with A and the other the ordering associated with $\overline{A}$. The Q value is associated with producing the optimal ordering with A, and $\overline{Q}$ value is associated with producing the worst-case ordering with $\overline{A}$.

Note that if the ranking is optimal, then Equation (4.11) can be simplified to this situation where $\overline{Q} = 0$ and thus

$$\mathrm{EPRD} = \mathcal{N}A + \frac{1}{2}. \tag{4.12}$$

This can serve as an approximation if one believes that the ranking that is being used is *nearly* optimal, which may be the case in some circumstances. However, if ranking is far from optimal, then using Equation (4.11) will be much more accurate, and the need for accuracy may drive the extra effort needed to apply this equation.

4.4.1 BEST- AND WORST-CASE PERFORMANCE

Best Case   The best case for ordering using Q and $\overline{Q}$ is what occurs in Equation (4.12), that is, when $Q = 1$ and A is set to 0.

Worst Case   The worst case can be interpreted in one of two ways. If $Q = 0$, then one should consider inverting the ranking algorithm, just as if $A = 1$, then one could use the opposite ordering, possibly by inverting parameter values, to produce a weaker ranking.

The worst-case rational ordering could also occur when $Q = 1$ and the $A = 1$, producing an EPRD that is large.

The random rational ordering would occur when $Q = 0.5$ and the A value will be random, producing a random EPRD that is about half of the number of documents in the system being studied.

4.5 GENERAL DISCRETE SINGLE FEATURE DISTRIBUTION MODELS

One can develop a general model for retrieval performance that can be applied to documents, scientific data, and a range of other kinds of data.

The A component may be computed using the cumulative distribution as

$$A = 1 - \sum_{i=0}^{\infty} \left(C_i(D) - \frac{\Pr(d_i)}{2} \right) \Pr(d_i | \text{rel}). \tag{4.13}$$

The cumulative distribution function is denoted as

$$C_n(D) = \sum_{i=0}^{n} \Pr(d_i).$$

The cumulative function represents the sum of all the probability values from 0 up to n in random variable D, representing a set of document values.

4.5.1 BINARY FEATURE MODEL

Using the development with cumulative distributions above, we may derive A for the binary model as with Equation (4.3).

$$\begin{aligned} A &= 1 - \left[\left((1-t) - \frac{1-t}{2} \right) (1-p) + \left(1 - \frac{t}{2} \right) p \right] \\ &= \frac{1 - p + t}{2}. \end{aligned} \tag{4.14}$$

We find that Equation (4.14), derived from the A definition consistent with the cumulative distribution, is equivalent to Equation (4.3), suggesting that the cumulative model is correct, at least with binary distributions.

4.5.2 A SINGLE POISSON FEATURE

When data consists of items that randomly arrive or occur, such as how many people pick up a telephone to use it during a single period of time, or the number of occurrences of a certain term that exists in a document, such as a web page. We can view these terms as randomly arriving at the web page. The rate of arrival is denoted here as λ, the number of occurrences per time unit. The probability of d term occurrences may be denoted as

$$\Pr(d) = \frac{e^{-\lambda}\lambda^d}{d!}. \tag{4.15}$$

Using Equation (4.13), the A can be computed consistent with the assumptions of the Poisson distribution as

$$A = 1 - \sum_{i=0}^{\infty}\left(\sum_{j=0}^{i}\frac{e^{-\lambda}\lambda^j}{j!} - \frac{e^{-\lambda}\lambda^i}{2(i!)}\right)\frac{e^{-\lambda_r}\lambda_r^i}{i!}. \tag{4.16}$$

Here λ is the average frequency in all documents and λ_r is the average frequency in relevant documents.

4.6   GENERAL CONTINUOUS FEATURE DISTRIBUTION MODELS

A more general definition of A may be performed using a continuous model of

$$A = \int_{\mu_r}^{\infty}\Pr(j)\,j. \tag{4.17}$$

This function may also be defined as the *survival function*. Here one can define A in terms of the survival function as:

$$A = \mathcal{S}(\mu_r, \text{all}). \tag{4.18}$$

4.6.1   NORMAL DISTRIBUTION

The most commonly studied probability distribution in statistics courses is the normal or Gaussian distribution. The survival function associated with the normal distribution is calculated as:

$$\mathcal{S}(\mu_r, \text{all}) = 1 - \frac{1}{2}\left(1 + \text{Erf}\left(\frac{\mu_r - \mu_{\text{all}}}{\sqrt{2}\sigma^2}\right)\right), \tag{4.19}$$

where $\text{Erf}(x)$ is the error function one finds discussed in literature about the normal distribution, $\text{Erf}(x) = \frac{2}{\sqrt{\pi}}\int_0^x e^{-t^2}\,dt$.

4.7   ADVANCED MODELS OF Q

4.7.1   POINT PROBABILITIES

One can compute Q in a simple way when probabilities are point probabilities. This is when a probability is represented by a single number. One can compute

$$Q = \Pr(\mu_r > \mu, X, 1 \succ 0) + \Pr(\mu_r \le \mu, Y, 1 \preceq 0), \tag{4.20}$$

where X is the option used for this particular probability, as is Y. For best-case ranking, X is $\mu_r > \mu$ and Y is $\mu_r \leq \mu$. The first probability represents where documents with the feature of 1 are ordered before documents with the feature of 0, denoted as $1 \succ 0$, and the second probability represents where documents with a feature of 0 are retrieved before documents with a feature of 1, denoted as $1 \preceq 0$.

Example 4.8   Point Probabilities. Consider 4 different orderings, with associated term frequencies and relevance values:

Rel	Freq	Rel	Freq	Rel	Freq	Rel	Freq
1	1	1	1	1	1	0	1
1	1	1	1	0	0	0	1
1	0	0	0	1	0	1	0
0	0	1	0	0	0	0	0
$p = 2/3$	$t = 1/2$	$p = 2/3$	$t = 1/2$	$p = 1/2$	$t = 1/4$	$p = 0$	$t = 1/2$

The Q value here is $3/4$, as 3 of the 4 orderings do not conflict with optimal ordering. The fourth of the orderings provides a situation where $p < t$, and this ordering is not consistent with optimal ordering. Therefore, $Q = 3/4$.

4.7.2   DISTRIBUTION INSTEAD OF A POINT PROBABILITY

In other circumstances, p is described accurately by a probabilistic distribution. One might then compute:

$$Q = \min \left(\int_{\mu}^{\infty} f(x)dz, \int_{x}^{\infty} f(z)dz \right) + \min \left(\int_{0}^{\mu} f(x)dz, \int_{0}^{y} f(z)dz \right), \qquad (4.21)$$

where $f()$ might represent a distribution such as the beta distribution, and where x and y are model-dependent parameters. This can be simplified to:

$$Q = - \int_{\min(\mu,x)}^{\max(\mu,y)} f(z)dz. \qquad (4.22)$$

Example 4.9   Beta Distribution describes p. In the case where the beta distribution accurately describes p, then $x = \mu$ and $y = \mu$. In this case, $Q = 1$.

4.7.3   INACCURATE KNOWLEDGE ABOUT A DISTRIBUTION

In some circumstances, what one thinks is an accurate distribution is in fact inaccurate. Given the accurate distribution $g(x)$ and our estimate distribution $h(x)$, the latter probably being inaccurate, then one may estimate Q as

$$Q = \min \left(\int_{\mu}^{\infty} g(z)dz, \int_{x}^{\infty} h(z)dz \right) + \min \left(\int_{0}^{\mu} g(z)dz, \int_{0}^{y} h(z)dz \right). \qquad (4.23)$$

When $g(a) = h(a)$ and $x = \mu$ and $y = \mu$, then Equation (4.23) is the same as Equation (4.21).

The variables x and y have distribution specific values. Usually, if μ is the mean for the $g()$ distribution, then x is the μ value for the $h()$ distribution, and similarly, y serves as the μ value for the $h()$ distribution. Equation (4.23) shows the top part of the $g()$ distribution and x is the comparable cutoff for the top part of $h()$. The y component for $h()$ is the cutoff for the bottom part of $h()$.

4.8   PREDICTING PERFORMANCE WITH HIGH PRECISION RETRIEVAL

One can measure A for a subset of the documents, such as the first n documents in high-precision retrieval, just as one can for all the documents, as in high-recall retrieval.

Example 4.10 A may be computed for the first n documents. Consider $\mathcal{N} = 100$ documents, $r_1 + n_1 = 50$, the number which have the feature d. There are $R = 25$ relevant documents, and $r_1 = 20$ of them have the feature in question and $n_1 = 30$. The A value is computed from $p = \Pr(d|\mathrm{rel}) = 20/25$ and $t = \Pr(d) = 50/100$, producing an A of $(1 - p + t)/2 = (1 - 20/25 + 50/100)/2 = (70/100)/2 = 0.35$.

If we consider all 100 documents with optimal ranking ($Q = 1$), the EPRD may be computed as $\mathcal{N} \times A + 1/2$ or $100 \times 0.35 + 1/2 = 35.5$.

In some situations, it may be difficult or impossible to determine some of the parameters for the first n parameters. However, when the basic parameters (p and t) of the first $R + N$ documents are available, then the EPRD may be computed.

4.8.1 A CHANGING FOR DIFFERENT SEGMENTS OF AN ORDERING

One might ask whether A is a constant over the length of the ordered list of documents. In this case, limiting oneself to the first n documents, one would expect the same t and p values to occur, resulting in the same EPRD value. When the proportional density of relevant and all documents remains the same throughout the list of documents, then the constant A assumption is consistent with the data.

It is likely that the relevant documents are concentrated toward the beginning of the ordered list of documents. In this case, the ratio of the p value and the t value will grow as one moves forward in the list of ordered documents. The A value will decrease (improve) as one moves n further forward in the ordered list, and the A value will likely increase (worsen) as one moves n toward the end of the ordered list of documents. One can view A as the average over the range of possible A values from the front of the list to the A values at the end of the list.

Given a high-precision situation where only the first n documents are considered, the A value may be computed for these n values and the parameters of the p and t values. This allows both A and EPRD to be used as high-precision performance measures.

4.9 SUMMARY

Using one term in a query and noting its presence or absence in each document may serve as the basis for possibly the simplest Information Retrieval system. Performance may be studied retrospectively, moving through the retrieval process and then studying the performance, or one can predict the performance, using methods described in this chapter. The EPRD is predicted from multiple subcomponents. The value A represents the scaled EPRD assuming optimal ordering. How often will this optimal ordering be obtained? The Q variable represents the probability of optimal ordering, and thus may indicate whether A is accurate. By combining A and Q appropriately, the EPRD and the ASL can be predicted in a wide range of situations.

Next we examine how one can predict Information Retrieval performance with multiple terms.

CHAPTER 5

Performance with Multiple Binary Features

There are often relationships between features in queries and other features in documents. For example, one might search for the term *cat*, but the terms or phrases *feline*, *felis catus*, *tabby*, or *Siamese* might occur in useful web pages and documents that don't contain the term *cat*. Many users submit multiple term queries, and we need to be able to develop a multiple term Information Retrieval model that captures statistical dependencies between features if we are to expand beyond our useful but simple single term performance model.

The features in a multi-feature system may be described using the probability notation in Chapter 2 as well as common notation in probability theory. We use the symbol μ_i to represent the mean frequency for feature i, and the symbol $\sigma_{i,j}$ represents the covariance for a pair of feature variables i and j.

5.1 PARTIAL DEPENDENCE

Before examining how to compute the full statistical dependence between all features in a document, we begin by examining how to include limited amounts of dependence between features. If one can determine those features that will contribute disproportionately more dependence information, these dependencies may be those that should be included if we are limited as to how many dependencies or what types of dependencies may be included. Using all dependencies may be prohibitively expensive, and choosing some important dependencies to use may be a more cost-effective approach.

5.1.1 MAXIMUM SPANNING TREE

The Maximum Spanning Tree (MST) serves as a data structure that captures those relationships that are the most important. More precisely, the MST is a structure that places any given term adjacent to those terms about which it carries the most information, the Expected Mutual Information Measure (EMIM), which is computed as:

$$EMIM(i, j) = \sum_{i,j} \Pr(i, j) \log \frac{\Pr(i, j)}{\Pr(i) \Pr(j)}. \tag{5.1}$$

Terms are added to the MST when the term being added is that term that contains the most expected mutual information, $EMIM(i, j)$, between the term being included, term i, and a node on the MST, term j. The tree begins with an arbitrarily chosen term.

Consider a tree with five terms, v, w, x, y, and z. Figure 5.1 shows this MST built using the five values. We begin to build the tree with the arbitrarily chosen term v. We then begin adding terms, by considering which term has the highest EMIM with term v. If this is term w, then this will be added as a link to term v. Next we consider what terms have the highest EMIM with any of the terms on the tree, v and w, and if we find that x has the highest EMIM with w, then x will be added below w. Similarly, y needs to be added, and if it is most informative about w, it is added below w, just as x is below w. As with x and y, z has more EMIM about w than it has about any other term and is added below w.

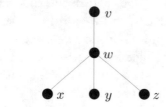

Figure 5.1: Maximum spanning tree.

Example 5.1   Assuming feature independence with the MST in Figure 5.1. Assume that we wish to compute the probability for finding the features w, x, and z together. This occurs when w, x, and z have the frequency of 1, while the other features, v and y, have frequency 0. The probability is computed as

$$
\begin{aligned}
\Pr(w = 1, x = 1, z = 1) \quad = \quad & \Pr(w = 1)\Pr(x = 1)\Pr(z = 1) \\
& \times \Pr(v = 0)\Pr(y = 0).
\end{aligned}
$$

Here the MST is not used in computing the joint probability. Instead, the joint probability is computed from the product of the independent probabilities for each of the five variables.

Example 5.2   Assuming feature dependence with the MST in Figure 5.1. Assume that we wish to compute the probability for finding the features w, x, and z together with frequency 1 and that features v and y have frequency 0. This is computed with dependencies from the MST as:

$$
\begin{aligned}
\Pr(w = 1, x = 1, z = 1) \quad = \quad & \Pr(v = 0)\Pr(w = 1|v = 0) \\
& \times \Pr(z = 1|w = 1)\Pr(y = 0|w = 1)\Pr(x = 1|w = 1).
\end{aligned}
$$

In this computation, we condition the value of each individual node given the node above it, or in the case of the top node, it is evaluated unconditionally. While this is not including all the possible relationships, such as that between x and y and between y and z, it includes those relationships that are expected to be the most important, as determined when the MST was constructed.

5.1.2   SIMPLE MAXIMUM SPANNING TREES

Figure 5.2 provides an MST where x is at the top of the tree and y is immediately below it, with these being the only two features present. The MST provides information about which feature is most related to which other feature and which feature is used to condition the probability of which other feature.

Figure 5.2: Maximum Spanning Tree with two nodes x and y.

Example 5.3   Independence with Figure 5.2. Consider that there are 3 documents, with profiles or characteristics $(0, 0)$, $(0, 1)$, and $(1, 1)$, with x being the first term and y the second term.

If we assume x and y are statistically independent, then

$$\Pr(x = 0, y = 0) = \Pr(x = 0)\Pr(y = 0) = \frac{2}{3}\frac{1}{3} = \frac{2}{9}.$$

Note that $2/9$ is not the correct answer; one of the three documents is $(0, 0)$, but $2/9$ is *close* to the correct answer, $1/3$.

Example 5.4   Dependence with Figure 5.2. If we assume dependence between the two features, then the probability of $(0, 0)$ is computed as

$$\Pr(x = 0, y = 0) = \Pr(x = 0)\Pr(y = 0|x = 0) = \frac{2}{3}\frac{1}{2} = \frac{1}{3}. \tag{5.2}$$

This is the correct answer.

$$\Pr(y = 0|x = 0) = \frac{1}{2}$$

because of the two documents with the first feature of 0, only one of the two has the second feature with a value of 0. We note here that using the full dependence here for the two features provides the exact, correct answer, whereas using statistical independence in the computation of joint probabilities produces an answer that may be close to the correct answer but is not the exact, correct answer.

Example 5.5   Three-Way Probabilities

Figure 5.3 shows two different MSTs for three different variables: x, y, and z. Figure 5.3a provides a tree where the relationships between x and y are included, as well as the relationship between y and z. In this case, the relationship between x and z is omitted. The relationship between z relates to y more strongly than z relates to x.

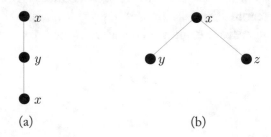

(a)   (b)

Figure 5.3: Maximum Spanning Tree.

Figure 5.3b shows a tree where x provides information about y and x provides information about z. The relationship between y and z is not included because y relates more strongly to x than it does to z, and z relates more strongly to x than it does to y.

Using either of the trees in Figure 5.3, some information is lost because some dependence information is omitted. Using dependence trees provides a representation of the strength of the relationships represented by adjacent tree nodes from which conditional probabilities can be produced.

5.1.3   PARTIAL DEPENDENCIES WITH BAHADUR LAZARSFELD AND GENERALIZED DEPENDENCE MODELS

While MSTs provide indicators of which dependencies are significant, other models may provide different forms of indicators. The Bahadur Lazarsfeld Expansion (BLE) [Losee, 1994] provides an algebraic and probabilistic estimation of probabilities, such as all n-way dependencies: all 2-way dependencies, all 3-way dependencies, all 4-way dependencies, and so forth, as well as the initial independence of features. By choosing how much dependence one wishes to include, one can choose only those degrees of dependence that are felt to be cost-effective for the application area.

One may move beyond the BLE to a more generalized model [Yu et al., 1983] and other approaches to provide some dependence information, which results in estimation performance that is usually superior to that with independence. Below are techniques useful for addressing more or all dependence information.

5.2 SINGULAR VALUE DECOMPOSITION

Consider the following five documents, each with three features: [{0, 1, 1}, {1, 0, 0}, {1, 1, 0}, {0, 1, 1}, {1, 1, 1}]. Note that the first and the fourth documents are duplicates. Each document represents the presence (1) or absence (0) of term 3, term 2, or term 1, moving from left to right across the number. One could consider the meaning of the terms, with the rightmost term as representing *corn*, the second (middle) term as *oats*, and the leftmost term as *wheat*.

The possible profiles are ordered from 0, 0, 0 up to 1, 1, 1 in traditional ascending binary ordering. The ordering of probabilities for the 8 possible profiles is [0.0, 0.0, 0.0, 0.4, 0.2, 0.0, 0.2, 0.2], which sums to 1. One may compute the probabilities for term 1, the rightmost feature, as [0.40, 0.60] for those features that have the values 0 and 1, respectively. This sums to 1. If we use the two rightmost features, the probabilities for the 4 possible feature profiles [{0, 0}, {0, 1}, {1, 0}, {1, 1}] will be: [0.2, 0.0, 0.2, 0.6], which sums to 1. We saw the probabilities for all 3 features above.

Using the data from above, one finds the following matrix with the three columns representing the three terms and the five rows representing the five documents:

$$\begin{pmatrix} 0.0 & 1.0 & 1.0 \\ 0.0 & 1.0 & 1.0 \\ 1.0 & 0.0 & 0.0 \\ 1.0 & 1.0 & 0.0 \\ 1.0 & 1.0 & 1.0 \end{pmatrix}.$$

One may be able to decompose this by using the Singular Value Decomposition method on this matrix. This produces 3 matrices: the U matrix, which is 5×5, the V matrix, which is 3×3, and the diagonal matrix D, which contains a row from the upper-left moving downward and rightward, representing values in the decomposed matrix that decrease in value.

$$U = \begin{pmatrix} -0.460 & 0.433 & 0.031 & -0.607 & -0.481 \\ -0.460 & 0.433 & 0.031 & 0.763 & -0.132 \\ -0.157 & -0.595 & -0.471 & 0.156 & -0.613 \\ -0.414 & -0.496 & 0.763 & 0 & 0 \\ -0.617 & -0.162 & -0.440 & -0.160 & 0.613 \end{pmatrix},$$

$$D = \begin{pmatrix} 2.753 & 0.0 & 0.0 \\ 0.0 & 1.451 & 0.0 \\ 0.0 & 0.0 & 0.560 \\ 0.0 & 0.0 & 0.0 \\ 0.0 & 0.0 & 0.0 \end{pmatrix}, \text{ and}$$

$$V = \begin{pmatrix} -0.431 & -0.863 & -0.264 \\ -0.709 & 0.143 & 0.691 \\ -0.558 & 0.485 & -0.673 \end{pmatrix}.$$

The original matrix can be regenerated by multiplying $U * D * transpose(V)$, which produces

$$Approximation = \begin{pmatrix} 0 & 1.0 & 1.0 \\ 0 & 1.0 & 1.0 \\ 1.0 & 0.0 & 0 \\ 1.0 & 1.0 & 0 \\ 1.0 & 1.0 & 1.0 \end{pmatrix}.$$

Note that this is an approximation of the earlier equation due to the numerical approximations made when computing the singular value decomposition and then putting it back together.

The values on the diagonal matrix D move from the largest value to the smallest value. One can simplify the system, producing a truncated matrix, by deciding that one wants to retain the most useful n features, and then the n features from the diagonal matrix D are kept and the other values to the lower right are set to 0, the n columns of U are retained (and the other n columns are discarded), and the n rows of V are retained (and other rows in V are discarded.) By producing an approximation of the original matrix, one obtains a simpler matrix. One can also do something like this, as is done in Latent Semantic Indexing, by zeroing out the values on the bottom right of the diagonal matrix, leaving the desired number of non-zero variances in D. Here is the D matrix with the bottom right (the third) value zeroed:

$$D = \begin{pmatrix} 2.753 & 0.0 & 0.0 \\ 0.0 & 1.451 & 0.0 \\ 0.0 & 0.0 & 0.0 \\ 0.0 & 0.0 & 0.0 \\ 0.0 & 0.0 & 0.0 \end{pmatrix}.$$

The result when these matrices are recombined is:

$$Approximation = \begin{pmatrix} 0.005 & 0.988 & 1.012 \\ 0.005 & 0.988 & 1.012 \\ 0.930 & 0.182 & -0.178 \\ 1.113 & 0.705 & 0.288 \\ 0.935 & 1.170 & 0.834 \end{pmatrix}.$$

When the approximation yields matrices with fractional values, one can round them to the nearest binary value.

5.3   TEUGELS' MODELS FOR FULL DEPENDENCE

Teugels [1990] has advanced our knowledge of the nature of multiple binary features and the dependencies between them. Many who have taken statistics courses are aware of logit or log-linear models, which can be used to capture binary dependent phenomena. Teugels provides some exact relationships based on feature vectors and Teugels' products, a generalization of the outer product denoted with $\otimes$, that allows us to compute related probabilities of features occurring with standard deviations and means for the data.

Teugels' [1990] models provide exact relationships between probabilities of multiple features and the covariance between them. By using these exact relationships, we can move from the individual probabilities to the covariance and average values, or from the covariance and average values to the probabilities. This will allow us to compute one set of values given another, and will allow us to change values, such as setting covariance values, to zero, to force independence between features.

5.3.1   COVARIANCES TO PROBABILITIES

Teugels [1990] suggests, for example, that one may convert from covariance values to probabilities by using the following:

$$
\begin{bmatrix}
p_{000} \\
p_{001} \\
p_{010} \\
p_{011} \\
p_{100} \\
p_{101} \\
p_{110} \\
p_{111}
\end{bmatrix}
=
\begin{bmatrix}
1 - p_3 & -1 \\
p_3 & 1
\end{bmatrix}
\otimes
\begin{bmatrix}
1 - p_2 & -1 \\
p_2 & 1
\end{bmatrix}
\otimes
\begin{bmatrix}
1 - p_1 & -1 \\
p_1 & 1
\end{bmatrix}
\begin{bmatrix}
1 \\
0 \\
0 \\
\sigma_{12} \\
0 \\
\sigma_{13} \\
\sigma_{23} \\
\theta
\end{bmatrix}. \tag{5.3}
$$

This may also be written more compactly using the following notation:

$$
\mathbf{p}^{(3)} =
\begin{bmatrix}
1 - p_i & -1 \\
p_i & 1
\end{bmatrix}^{\otimes(3)}
\begin{bmatrix}
1 \\
0 \\
0 \\
\sigma_{12} \\
0 \\
\sigma_{13} \\
\sigma_{23} \\
\theta
\end{bmatrix}, \tag{5.4}
$$

where the matrix raised to the $\otimes(3)$ (superscript) power represents the matrix from p_3 down to p_1 with multiplication using the Kronecker product ($\otimes$). Here σ_{ij} represents the covariance between feature i and feature j, and θ represents the covariance between all three features. The vector $\mathbf{p}^{(3)} = (p_{000}, p_{001}, p_{010}, p_{011}, p_{100}, p_{101}, p_{110}, p_{111})^T$. Using the above equations, one is able to derive, from a vector of covariance values, the probabilities for the data. Below we will see the reverse computation, where we move from the probabilities to the covariance values.

5.3.2 AVERAGES TO PROBABILITIES

The probabilities describing the data may be produced from average values μ with the following operations:

$$\mathbf{p}^{(2)} = \begin{bmatrix} 1 & -1 \\ 0 & 1 \end{bmatrix} \otimes \begin{bmatrix} 1 & -1 \\ 0 & 1 \end{bmatrix} \begin{bmatrix} 1 \\ p_1 \\ p_2 \\ \mu_{12} \end{bmatrix}. \tag{5.5}$$

Equation (5.5) allows one to move from the averages, or expected values, to the probabilities. Below, we will be able to move from the probabilities to the average values, essentially the opposite direction from Equation (5.5).

5.3.3 PROBABILITIES TO COVARIANCES

One may convert from a probability vector to the covariance values by computing the dot product of the conversion array times the probability, producing the covariance array:

$$\begin{bmatrix} 1 \\ 0 \\ 0 \\ \sigma_{12} \end{bmatrix} = \begin{bmatrix} 1 & 1 \\ -p_2 & 1-p_2 \end{bmatrix} \otimes \begin{bmatrix} 1 & 1 \\ -p_1 & 1-p_1 \end{bmatrix} \mathbf{p}^{(2)}. \tag{5.6}$$

Using Equation (5.6) allows one to convert from the probabilities, representing the feature probabilities, to generate the covariance data, indicating the covariance between features.

5.3.4 PROBABILITIES TO AVERAGES

One may compute the average values, μ, from probabilities with:

$$\begin{bmatrix} 1 \\ p_1 \\ p_2 \\ \mu_{12} \end{bmatrix} = \begin{bmatrix} 1 & 1 \\ 0 & 1 \end{bmatrix}^{\otimes(2)} [p_{00}, p_{01}, p_{10}, p_{11}]^T. \tag{5.7}$$

This allows one to compute the average values, or μ values, from the probabilities.

These four conversions are valuable in manipulating probabilities, covariance values, and averages or expected values. One can convert from the average values to probabilities (Equation (5.5) above) (Teugels [1990, p. 260, Equation 2.5]), from probabilities to averages (Equation (5.7) above) (Teugels [1990, p. 260, Equation 2.6]), from probabilities to covariances (Equation (5.6) above) (Teugels [1990, p. 260, Equation 2.8]), and from covariances to probabilities (Equation (5.3) above) (Teugels [1990, p. 260, Equation 2.7]).

5.4   EXAMPLE WITH DOCUMENTS

Using the documents and probabilities in Section 5.2 on Page 37, we can apply Teugels' models, as described earlier, to see how to compute probabilities, means, and covariance values for this data.

Example 5.6   Probabilities to Averages with One Binary Term. Converting from the probability to the μ values is computed using Equation (5.7), using only the first feature:

$$\begin{bmatrix} 1.0 \\ 0.6 \end{bmatrix} = \begin{bmatrix} 1 & 1 \\ 0 & 1 \end{bmatrix} \begin{bmatrix} 0.4 \\ 0.6 \end{bmatrix}.$$

Example 5.7   Probabilities to Averages with Two Binary Terms. If we wish to examine the two rightmost features, we can compute the averages for these two features as:

$$\begin{bmatrix} 1.0 \\ 0.6 \\ 0.8 \\ 0.6 \end{bmatrix} = \begin{bmatrix} 1 & 1 \\ 0 & 1 \end{bmatrix} \otimes \begin{bmatrix} 1 & 1 \\ 0 & 1 \end{bmatrix} \begin{bmatrix} 0.2 \\ 0.0 \\ 0.2 \\ 0.6 \end{bmatrix}.$$

Example 5.8   Probabilities to Averages with Three Binary Terms. The averages for these three binary terms may be computed from the probabilities using the following:

$$\begin{bmatrix} 1.0 \\ 0.6 \\ 0.8 \\ 0.6 \\ 0.6 \\ 0.2 \\ 0.4 \\ 0.2 \end{bmatrix} = \begin{bmatrix} 1 & 1 \\ 0 & 1 \end{bmatrix}^{\otimes(3)} \begin{bmatrix} 0.0 \\ 0.0 \\ 0.0 \\ 0.4 \\ 0.2 \\ 0.0 \\ 0.2 \\ 0.2 \end{bmatrix}.$$

The averages for the rightmost, the rightmost two, and all three features are computed from the corresponding probabilities.

Example 5.9   Averages to Probabilities with One Binary Term. The probabilities may be computed from the averages (μ values) using the data at the start of this section:

$$\begin{bmatrix} 0.4 \\ 0.6 \end{bmatrix} = \begin{bmatrix} 1 & -1 \\ 0 & 1 \end{bmatrix} \begin{bmatrix} 1 \\ 0.6 \end{bmatrix}. \tag{5.8}$$

Example 5.10   Averages to Probabilities with Two Binary Terms. The probabilities may be computed using the values for the first (or rightmost) two binary terms or features:

$$
\begin{bmatrix} 0.2 \\ 0.0 \\ 0.2 \\ 0.6 \end{bmatrix} = \begin{bmatrix} 1 & -1 \\ 0 & 1 \end{bmatrix} \otimes \begin{bmatrix} 1 & -1 \\ 0 & 1 \end{bmatrix} \begin{bmatrix} 1.0 \\ 0.6 \\ 0.8 \\ 0.6 \end{bmatrix}. \tag{5.9}
$$

Example 5.11   Averages to Probabilities with Three Binary Terms. Continuing, all three features in the original dataset may be used in computing the probabilities for the $2^3 = 8$ combinations of the 3 binary features:

$$
\begin{bmatrix} 0.0 \\ 0.0 \\ 0.0 \\ 0.4 \\ 0.2 \\ 0.0 \\ 0.2 \\ 0.2 \end{bmatrix} = \begin{bmatrix} 1 & -1 \\ 0 & 1 \end{bmatrix}^{\otimes(3)} \begin{bmatrix} 1.0 \\ 0.6 \\ 0.8 \\ 0.6 \\ 0.6 \\ 0.2 \\ 0.4 \\ 0.2 \end{bmatrix}. \tag{5.10}
$$

Example 5.12   Probabilities to Covariances with One Binary Term. The covariances may be computed from the probabilities for one initial term, using Equation (5.6):

$$
\begin{bmatrix} 1.0 \\ 0.0 \end{bmatrix} = \begin{bmatrix} 1 & 1 \\ -p_1 & 1 - p_1 \end{bmatrix} \begin{bmatrix} 0.4 \\ 0.6 \end{bmatrix}. \tag{5.11}
$$

Example 5.13   Probabilities to Covariances with Two Binary Terms. Continuing with two binary features, the probabilities may be computed from the covariances as

$$
\begin{bmatrix} 1.0 \\ 0.0 \\ 0.0 \\ 0.12 \end{bmatrix} = \begin{bmatrix} 1 & 1 \\ -p_2 & 1 - p_2 \end{bmatrix} \otimes \begin{bmatrix} 1 & 1 \\ -p_1 & 1 - p_1 \end{bmatrix} \begin{bmatrix} 0.2 \\ 0.0 \\ 0.2 \\ 0.6 \end{bmatrix}. \tag{5.12}
$$

Example 5.14   Probabilities to Covariances with Three Binary Terms. Using all three features from the original dataset, the exact covariance values may be computed from the probabilities as:

$$
\begin{bmatrix} 1.0 \\ 0.0 \\ 0.0 \\ 0.12 \\ 0.0 \\ -0.16 \\ -0.08 \\ 0.016 \end{bmatrix} = \begin{bmatrix} 1 & 1 \\ -p_i & 1 - p_i \end{bmatrix}^{\otimes(3)} \begin{bmatrix} 0.0 \\ 0.0 \\ 0.0 \\ 0.4 \\ 0.2 \\ 0.0 \\ 0.2 \\ 0.2 \end{bmatrix}. \tag{5.13}
$$

Example 5.15   Covariances to Probabilities with One Binary Term. Using Equation (5.3), one can compute the initial probability for the rightmost feature from the covariances for the rightmost feature as:

$$
\begin{bmatrix} 0.4 \\ 0.6 \end{bmatrix} = \begin{bmatrix} 1 - p_1 & -1 \\ p_1 & 1 \end{bmatrix} \begin{bmatrix} 1.0 \\ 0.0 \end{bmatrix}. \tag{5.14}
$$

Example 5.16   Covariances to Probabilities with Two Binary Terms. Given covariances based on two rightmost feature values, the probabilities may be computed:

$$
\begin{bmatrix} 0.2 \\ 0.0 \\ 0.2 \\ 0.6 \end{bmatrix} = \begin{bmatrix} 1 - p_i & -1 \\ p_i & 1 \end{bmatrix}^{\otimes(2)} \begin{bmatrix} 1.0 \\ 0.0 \\ 0.0 \\ 0.12 \end{bmatrix}. \tag{5.15}
$$

Example 5.17   Covariances to Probabilities with Three Binary Terms. We may continue with three-way covariances being used to compute the probabilities:

$$
\begin{bmatrix} 0.0 \\ 0.0 \\ 0.0 \\ 0.4 \\ 0.2 \\ 0.0 \\ 0.2 \\ 0.2 \end{bmatrix} = \begin{bmatrix} 1 - p_i & -1 \\ p_i & 1 \end{bmatrix}^{\otimes(3)} \begin{bmatrix} 1.0 \\ 0.00 \\ 0.0 \\ 0.12 \\ 0.00 \\ -0.16 \\ -0.08 \\ 0.016 \end{bmatrix}. \tag{5.16}
$$

5.5 PREDICTING PERFORMANCE WITH FEATURE DEPENDENCE

We may compute the EPRD whether terms are independent or dependent. Assuming statistical dependence of features and optimal ranking, one may compute the EPRD easily using

$$EPRD = \mathcal{N}A + \frac{1}{2}. \tag{5.17}$$

Equation (4.18) shows that

$$A = \mathcal{S}(\mu_r, \text{all}).$$

A may be computed by summing the probability function for all the documents from the position of the average relevant document.

To perform this, we need to sort all different document positions from the highest probability of the document characteristics, given that they are relevant, to the lowest value, given that they are relevant. From this, one can then sum or integrate over all positions from the average position of a relevant document to the highest possible position. Thus, we can compute

$$A = \sum_{i=\mu_r}^{n} \Pr(d_i|\text{rel})Pos(d_i|\text{all}),$$

where $Pos(x)$ represents the middle position of documents with x. Given this A value, one can compute the EPRD by multiplying by the number of documents $\mathcal{N}$ by A and then adding $1/2$.

Example 5.18 Dependence and EPRD. Using the example proposed above in Section 5.4 on Page 41, we can see that the original order (essentially unordered documents) can be changed to the following.

Profile	Rel	Non-rel	$\Pr(d|rel)$	$\Pr(d)$	$Pos(d|All)$	$\Pr(d|rel)\ Pos(d|All)$
000	0	1	0	1/10	19/20	0
010	0	1	0	1/10	17/20	0
011	2	1	2/5	3/10	13/20	13/50
100	1	1	1/5	2/10	8/20	2/25
110	1	0	1/5	1/10	5/20	1/20
111	1	1	1/5	2/10	2/20	1/50

Using the data in the rightmost column, we can see that the sum of the expected probabilities is $41/100$ and thus the average position of a relevant document is $A = 0.41$.

5.6 VALIDATION

Does our method for computing dependencies work as described in an Information Retrieval context? We can test this by comparing actual rankings and probabilities with predicted values using the software at `http://ils.unc.edu/~losee/irv`. If the predictions match with actual probabilities and rankings, then we may conclude that the methods for addressing estimates of dependencies are accurate.

Using all possible 1-, 2-, 3-, and 4-way dependencies and all possible sets of documents that might exist with 1 to 10 documents, the system produced 551,370 results, and all 551,370 were accurate estimates, suggesting that the method works correctly. The validation system computes the EPRD for each of the sets of documents and then it compares this to the ASL computed from the empirical ordering of the set of documents. The prediction is considered to be correct if the ASL and the EPRD are within 0.001 of each other to address rounding errors that occur with calculations. Making half a million predictions and finding them to all be correct is a strong finding, but we could obviously use more dependencies or more documents for each document set. For purposes here, we considered a half-million tests sufficient for the analysis of these procedures, but those trying to make a stronger argument might wish to try more dependencies and more documents.

5.7 FEATURE INDEPENDENCE

Statistical dependence and the EPRD may be calculated, but with the probabilities calculated from the covariance values used to achieve independence. The fractional covariance values between features must be set to zero and then the probabilities calculated, and then the EPRD computed.

Example 5.19   Term Independence. Using the preceding example, one can try to view the relevant documents as though they were statistically dependent. The covariance array for the three terms is

$$
\begin{bmatrix} 1.0 \\ 0.00 \\ 0.0 \\ 0.12 \\ 0.00 \\ -0.16 \\ -0.08 \\ 0.016 \end{bmatrix},
\tag{5.18}
$$

as was shown above. The covariance values for relationships between terms may be set to 0, because "X_1 and X_2 will be independent iff $\sigma_{1,2} = 0$" [Teugels, 1990, p. 257], producing the following covariance vector:

$$[1, 0, 0, 0, 0, 0, 0, 0]^T,$$

which is used with independent features. Note that the 1 is always used and represents a constant in the independence covariance vector.

Using Equation (5.3), one may compute the probabilities that are consistent with term independence. One can compute the EPRD by computing the A value with

$$
\begin{bmatrix} 0.0 \\ 0.0 \\ 0.0 \\ 0.4 \\ 0.2 \\ 0.0 \\ 0.2 \\ 0.2 \end{bmatrix} = \begin{bmatrix} 1 - p_i & -1 \\ p_i & 1 \end{bmatrix}^{\otimes (3)} \begin{bmatrix} 1.0 \\ 0.00 \\ 0.00 \\ 0.00 \\ 0.00 \\ 0.00 \\ 0.00 \\ 0.00 \end{bmatrix}, \tag{5.19}
$$

and this may be used in computing the document ranking or the EPRD consistent with statistical independence of features.

5.8   SUMMARY

The performance obtained, addressing only a single term, was developed in Chapter 4. In this chapter, we examined relationships between terms as far as whether the terms are statistically independent or statistically dependent. These relationships can address some limited statistical information provided by some features about some other features, or one can address all possible relationships. One can exactly predict the EPRD with full statistical dependence, or one can estimate the EPRD, with some error being incurred, when only partial information is available.

The more terms or features are involved, the more computationally expensive will be the computation of EPRD. Because of this, it is often desired to use a subset of all possible dependencies, producing estimates containing errors rather than the accurate but time-consuming computation of an exact EPRD.

CHAPTER 6

Applications: Metadata and Linguistic Labels

6.1 METADATA AND INDEXING

Metadata represents *data about data*, as it is commonly described. Serving as representations of the nature of the data that the metadata describes, it can serve to provide index terminology in document systems, or it may provide information about items in retail outlets, such as vegetables in a grocery store. In the case of retail and wholesale vendors, there may be extensive standards developed as to how to use and apply the metadata. Metadata may also be studied as *metainformation*, or as information about information. Because of information theory, the rigorous study of information and information-theoretic relations between variables, metainformation may be studied equally rigorously [Losee, 2013b].

Index terms or phrases function as metadata does, representing topical information and other characteristics. Index terms are often used to represent document features, while metadata may be similarly used or may be applied to representations other than information. Index terms may represent the topic that the language in a book describes, while metadata is often used to describe products, such as items in a grocery store or inventory produced by a manufacturing plant.

The choice to apply metadata may be based upon decision-theoretic considerations, and we will examine these below. By using a performance measure consistent with certain parameters, we can see when performance improves or decreases, and one can then examine the parameters in this situation, possibly determining when certain parameters under our control are shifted so as to improve performance.

We know that through the application of Equation (4.11) on Page 27, the following EPRD for a single binary term may be developed as

$$\text{EPRD} = \mathcal{N}\left[QA + \overline{Q}\,\overline{A}\right] + 1/2.$$ (6.1)

This assumes that Q is two-valued and that we have a single metadata term. We can expand Equation (6.1) if we wish to add index terms or metadata. The EPRD without adding a term is

$$\text{EPRD} = (R + N)\left[(1 - (r_1/R) + (r_1 + n_1)/(R + N))/2\right] + 1/2,$$ (6.2)

where $p = r_1/R$ and $t = (r_1 + n_1)/(R + N)$. We assume here that the values R and N are the same both before and after assigning or changing terms. The variables r_1 and n_1 are modified in the discussion below by adding to r_1 or n_1 or subtracting from either of these variables.

6.1.1 ASSIGNING TERMS TO RELEVANT DOCUMENTS

Before adding a term, Equation (6.2) can be viewed as $(R + N) [(1 - (r_1/R) + (r_1 + n_1)/(R + N))/2] + 1/2$ and, after a metadata term has been added, this becomes

$$\text{EPRD} = (R + N) [(1 - ((r_1 + 1)/R) + (r_1 + 1 + n_1)/(R + N))/2] + 1/2. \tag{6.3}$$

This improves the EPRD (Equation (6.2)) by the quantity $+(N/R)/2$ from the EPRD (Equation (6.3)). By determining what the difference is between performance with term presence and term absence, we can determine when and how adding a term is a good choice.

6.1.2 NOT ASSIGNING TERMS TO RELEVANT DOCUMENTS

We can similarly address what happens when a metadata term is not assigned to a relevant document. The EPRD worsens by $-(N/R)/2$, decreasing performance.

6.1.3 NOT ASSIGNING TERMS TO NON-RELEVANT DOCUMENTS

If we choose to not assign a query term to a non-relevant document, we find that the EPRD improves by $1/2$.

6.1.4 INCORRECTLY ASSIGNING TERMS TO NON-RELEVANT DOCUMENT

If we incorrectly assign the term to a non-relevant document, the EPRD worsens by $-1/2$.

The results of these four different options of correctness and adding or not adding terms is summarized in the top part of Table 6.1.

Example 6.1 The bottom part of Table 6.1 provides an example showing the application of the rules and formulas in the top part of the table. Given documents with the parameters $N = 80$, $R = 20$, $n_1 = 5$, and $r_1 = 15$, the numeric changes in EPRD occur when terms are added or not added to relevant or non-relevant documents, given the data on Page 49.

6.2 VALIDATING METADATA RULES

One validating study iterated through 1 to 14 documents, applying the rules in the first several lines of Table 6.1, with simulations validating that the rules were accurate [Losee, 2013]. For this large range of document sizes, does performance improve or decrease when a term is added or removed? Software made 2, 328, 410 predictions, iterating through different orderings for 1 document, 2 documents, through 14 documents, and *all* predictions were found to agree with what

Table 6.1: Metadata inclusion criteria

Positive IMA Values Represent Improvements (Decreased EPRD)	Assignment of Term for Relevant Documents	Relevant Documents not Assigned Term	Non-Relevant Document Removing Assigned Term	Non-Relevant Document Incorrectly Assigned Term
Effect	Improves	Worsens	Improves	Worsens
Optimal ranking ($Q = 1$)	$(N/R)/2$	$-(N/R)/2$	$+1/2$	$-1/2$
$Q<1$	$(1/2)(2NQ-N)/R$	$(1/2)(2NQ-N)/R$	$Q - 1/2$	$-Q + 1/2$
Below: Indexing and Metadata When $N = 80$, $R = 20$, $n_1 = 5$, and $r_1 = 15$				
$Q = 1$	2	-2	$+1/2$	$-1/2$
$Q = 0.8$	$6/5$	$-6/5$	$+3/10$	$-3/10$

actually happens when compared to real documents generated iteratively [Losee, 2013]. The software is publicly available (`http://ils.unc.edu/~losee/ima`) and can be used to replicate tests and can be modified to experiment with different assumptions.

Do the rules examined always accurately describe what occurs? This validation technique might fail when the number of documents exceeds 14 documents, but it seems unlikely. The validation studies show that, for all possible combinations from 1 document up to 14 documents, the methods described here work accurately. The author is not aware of any ordering phenomena that would be different above 14 documents than it would in the range of 5 to 10 documents. This suggests that the rules, when applied exhaustively to a reasonable range of document sizes, predict accurately, supporting the idea that the rules are correct.

6.3   NATURAL LANGUAGE PART-OF-SPEECH TAGS

While metadata tags represent the presence or absence of a certain feature that is associated with data features, natural language features are known and understood by many of the speakers of the language, largely due to formal education. Natural languages may assign part-of-speech tags, such as *noun*, *verb*, or *adjective*. Other tags may represent different meanings for a term. The term *bank* might refer to a financial institution, which we will call meaning (1), or *bank* may refer to the side of a river or a stream, which we will refer to as meaning (2). Both of these are nouns, yet they mean different things, and the term "number" serves to provide *word sense disambiguation.* Attaching a meaning number to each term will make the term more precise, disambiguating it.

One might ask the question whether A be improved (smaller) with tags rather than without the tags. Thus, we will be looking for a situation where A with tags is less than A without tags:

$$A_{\text{Tags}} < A_{\text{WithoutTags}}. \tag{6.4}$$

We can expand this question and simplify to:

$$1 + \tau t - \pi p < 1 + t - p. \tag{6.5}$$

As before, t represents the probability that the term occurs in a document, $\Pr(d)$, and p represents the probability that the term occurs in a relevant document, or $\Pr(d|\text{rel})$. The variable τ is the probability that the tag will be added to a term, given that it has the term, and π is the probability that the tag will be added to the term, given that it has the term in a relevant document. By assuming independence between the tags and the probabilities of occurrences, we can calculate the joint probabilities of relevance and non-relevance as $p \times \pi$ and $t \times \tau$.

The degree to which A without tags exceeds A with tags may be referred to as the *Tag Improvement Factor.* By using the Tag Improvement Factor comparing the ASL or A with tags vs. the ASL or A without the tags, one can learn how much of a performance difference exists with tags added. One may then be able to answer questions about whether adding a tag is worthwhile and cost-effective.

Example 6.2 Example Assuming Tag Independence. Consider a situation as in this table:

	Relevant Documents	All Documents
All Terms	100	1,000
With Term x	50	100
Term x is Noun	30	50

where there are 100 documents that are relevant, 50 relevant documents with term x, and 1000 documents overall, with 100 documents with term x. In this case, $p = 50/100 = 1/2$ and $t = 100/1000 = 1/10$. Thus, $A = (1 - p + t)/2 = (1 - 1/2 + 1/10)/2 = (20/20 - 10/20 + 2/20)/2 = 6/20$.

Let us also assume that 30 of the 50 relevant documents with the term are also labeled as *nouns* and 50 of the 100 documents overall with the term are labeled as *nouns*. In this case, $\pi = 30/50 = 3/5$ and $\tau = 50/100 = 1/2$. Our decision case now becomes, assuming independence and using Equation (6.5), that something should be labeled as a *noun* if and only if A with tags is less than A without tags:

$$1 - (50/100 \times 30/50) + (1/10 \times 1/2) \quad < \quad 1 - 1/2 + 1/10.$$
$$(1 - 15/50 + 1/4) = 0.95 \quad < \quad 6/10.$$

This is *false* and suggests that performance is worse when the tagging is incorporated given these parameters and assuming independence of the parameters.

Example 6.3   Example Assuming Dependence. We remove the assumption of statistical independence, and we assume that all relevant documents with the term are nouns and that all documents with the terms are nouns. The dependent combination of p and π is 30/100 and t and τ is 50/1000. Thus, one might calculate $A = (1 - 30/100 + 50/1000)/2 = 0.3525$.

6.3.1   BEST- AND WORST-CASE PERFORMANCE WITH TAGS

Best-Case Performance   Best-case performance consistent with statistical independence is obtained when the $A = (1 - p + t)/2$ value is at its minimum. This occurs when p increases and t decreases, with both approaching the extreme values of $p \to 1$ and $t \to 0$.

When one has the expanded version of A with tags, we want to minimize $A = (1 - \pi p + \tau t)/2$. In this case, it is necessary to maximize the product πp and thus the value of the individual components π and p, as well as minimize the product τt and thus minimize both its components τ and t.

Example 6.4   Assume that we have 10 documents with 5 relevant, with 6 of the documents having the feature in question and 4 of the relevant documents having the feature in question. We also assume independence of part-of-speech tag probabilities and the probability of occurrence for the parts of speech. The best case for A is obtained with the minimum value for τt and the maximum value for πp. Since $t = 6/10$, a $\tau = 0.0$ would bring the product τt down to approximately 0.0. Attempting to maximize πp where $p = 4/5$, setting $\pi = 1$ results in the product $1 \times 4/5 = 4/5$. The best (minimum) A value would then be $A_{\text{bestcase}} = (1 - (1(4/5)) + (0(6/10)))/2 = (1 - 4/5 + 0)/2 = 1/10$.

Worst-Case Performance   Worst-case performance will be the inverse of the above, where $A = (1 - \pi p + \tau t)/2$. We thus need π and p at their minimum and τ and t at their maximum.

6.4   SUMMARY

Besides examining document retrieval performance by looking at the probabilistic parameters associated with document terms, one may examine additional characteristics. Metadata and index terms can be used to provide additional or replacement features in lieu of terminology. The decisions to choose to use a certain index term or to assign metadata expressions can be based upon decision-theoretic considerations, where we assign an index term or assign metadata when it decreases the cost compared to not assigning the term.

Part-of-speech tags can be used to assist in disambiguating terminology. By choosing those tags that improve expected performance, one can improve retrieval with natural language information.

CHAPTER 7

Conclusion

Information Retrieval systems attempt to take features supplied by a user as a query and locate those documents in a database that are similar to the topics mentioned in the query, with some systems attempting to answer questions. While several different models of identifying which documents should be retrieved have been proposed, we have focused above on probabilistic methods. By ordering documents based upon their probability of relevance, documents that are relevant will be near the front of the ordered list of documents. The arrangements may be described graphically or mathematically in terms of a number of measures of Information Retrieval performance.

While most Information Retrieval studies examine retrospective performance that is available after Information Retrieval processes have identified documents, the emphasis in this work is on predicting performance before documents have been retrieved. While search lengths have been studied in the past, we suggest the ASL may, in turn, be predicted using analytic methods. The EPRD may be predicted based on probabilities; there is no need to develop an experimental system and test how existing documents are retrieved with this existing system. Note that there are not obvious ways of addressing the prediction of most other measures.

Chapter 4 provides techniques for predicting the EPRD assuming that there is only a single term in the query and in documents. Documents may have more than the term in question, but only this single binary query term is addressed in this simple Information Retrieval process. Interestingly, some portions of the prediction method can be accurate with several different probabilistic models for the term distributions, such as the binary or Bernoulli distribution or the Poisson distribution, which are useful for the number of terms in documents, or the normal distribution, which may capture the variation in data that is being retrieved.

Multiple terms exist in natural language text, and clearly developing Information Retrieval performance models consistent with multiple terms is highly desirable. Beginning with single terms allowed us to view simple relationships, which can then lead to more complex models, such as with multiple terms. We begin with some models of how to predict probabilities with only certain dependencies between multiple terms. By selecting a limited number of dependencies, instead of all of the relationships, the system allows for the set of probabilities to include only those most useful probabilities. By computing all dependencies, we can produce perfectly accurate probabilities. Using all dependencies may involve using a simple model that allows us to understand what relationships and characteristics produce what level of performance. This multiple term model has been validated through large numbers of simulations, which generate an accurate prediction of the ordering of documents across a wide range of possible documents.

Additional information may be studied as it supplements the Information Retrieval process with natural language terms. Will index terms be appropriate in certain circumstances? A rule for the inclusion of metadata and index terms is developed which tells us when to include a term with certain characteristics. This is applicable to both metadata features and to index terms for retrieval of documents. One may also add certain characteristics to language features. For example, is knowing the part of speech of a certain term useful, and how can this be used, and when?

Information Retrieval may be viewed as an application domain of computer science, and we suggest that Information Retrieval would be better treated as a science, as are some other areas of computer science, such as algorithms and formal language theory. In earlier chapters, methods are suggested for determining performance given certain system parameters. Most sciences produce rules predicting outcomes consistent with system characteristics. Many of us learn rules in chemistry and in physics classes, perhaps describing the laws relating volume, pressure, and temperature of gases, or a law relating distance traveled as computed from velocity and time. Similarly, Information Retrieval can have rules or laws that describe how the systems perform.

The purpose of this work has been to suggest some basic relationships between parameters of document sets and the Information Retrieval performance that is obtained with the parameters. Simple models are suggested, assuming only one term, as well as more complex multiple term models. These models make accurate predictions, and can serve as steppingstones toward the further development of a science of Information Retrieval.

APPENDIX A

Variables

Variable	Meaning
A	Scaled Expected Position of a Relevant Document
$\overline{A}$	$1 - A$
all	Set of all documents
ASL	Average Search Length
d	document with feature frequency 1
$\overline{d}$	document with feature frequency 0
$d_{n,0}$	non-relevant document without the feature in question
$d_{n,1}$	non-relevant document with the feature in question
$d_{r,0}$	relevant document without the feature in question
$d_{r,1}$	relevant document with the feature in question
EPRD	Expected Position of a Relevant Document
$\mathcal{N}$	Number of documents
N	Number of non-relevant documents
N_{ret}	Number of non-relevant that have been retrieved
n_1	Number of non-relevant documents with the feature
p	$\Pr(d|\text{rel})$
$\Pr(d_i|\text{rel})$	Probability a relevant document has feature i
Q	probability of optimal ordering
$\overline{Q}$	$1 - Q$
R	Number of relevant documents
R_{ret}	Number of relevant documents that have been retrieved
r_1	Number of relevant documents with the feature
rel	Set of relevant documents
t	Probability a term is in a document, $\Pr(d|\text{all})$

Bibliography

Bookstein, Abraham. Information retrieval: A sequential learning process, *Journal of the American Society for Information Science*, vol. 34, no. 4, pp. 331–342, 1983. DOI: 10.1002/asi.4630340504. 6

Church, Lewis. Combinatoric models of information retrieval: Ranking methods and performance measures for weakly-ordered document collections, Ph.D. Dissertation, University of North Carolina, Chapel Hill, 2010. https://cdr.lib.unc.edu/indexablecontent/uuid:252c9f52-ca31--4206-930b-e97b5742efb1 5, 22, 24, 26

Cleverdon, Cyril. The cranfield tests on index language devices, *Aslib Proceedings*, vol. 19 no. 6, pp. 173–194, 1967. https://doi.org/10.1108/eb050097 DOI: 10.1108/eb050097. 11

Cooper, William S. Expected search length: A single measure of retrieval effectiveness based on the weak ordering action of retrieval systems, *Journal of the American Society for Information Science*, vol. 19, no. 1, pp. 30–41, 1968. DOI: 10.1002/asi.5090190108. 18

Fritsch, Rudolf and Fritsch, Gerda. *The Four Color Theorem: History Topological Foundations, and Idea of Proof*, Springer-Verlag, New York, 1998. DOI: 10.1007/978-1-4612-1720-6. 2

Losee, Robert M. Term dependence: Truncating the Bahadur Lazarsfeld expansion, *Information, Processing, and Management*, vol. 30, no. 2, pp. 293–303, 1994. DOI: 10.1016/0306-4573(94)90071-x. 36

Losee, Robert M. *Text Retrieval and Filtering*, Kluwer, Norwell, MA, 1998. DOI: 10.1007/978-1-4615-5705-0.

Losee, Robert M. The effect of assigning a metadata or indexing term on document ordering, *Journal of the American Society for Information Science and Technology*, vol. 64, no. 11, pp. 2191–2200, 2013. DOI: 10.1002/asi.22919. 48, 49

Losee, Robert M. Informational facts and the metainformation inherent in IFacts: The soul of data sciences, *Journal of Library Metadata*, vol. 13, issue 1, pp. 59–74, 2013b. DOI: 10.1080/19386389.2013.778732. 47

Manning, Christopher D., Raghavan, Prabhakar, and Schutze, Heinrich. *Introduction to Information Retrieval*, Cambridge University Press, 2008. DOI: 10.1017/cbo9780511809071. 11

Meng, Xiannong and Clark, Ty. An empirical user rating of popular search engines using RankPower, *Proc. of the International Conference on Information Technology: Coding and Computing*, vol. 2, pp. 521–525, 2005. DOI: 10.1109/itcc.2005.76. 19

Meng, Xiannong. A comparative study of performance measures for information retrieval systems, *Proc. of the 3rd International Conference on Information Technology: New Generations, IEEE Computer Science Society*, pp. 578–579, Washington DC, 2006. DOI: 10.1109/itng.2006.2. 19

Raghavan, Vijay V., Jung, Gwang S., and Bollmann, Peter. A critical investigation of recall and precision as measures of retrieval system performance, *ACM Transactions on Information Systems*, vol. 7, no. 3, pp. 205–229, July 1989. DOI: 10.1145/65943.65945. 13

Robertson, Stephen E. and Sparck Jones, Karen. Relevance weighting of search terms, *Journal of the American Society for Information Science*, vol. 27, issue 3, pp. 129–146, May 1976. DOI: 10.1002/asi.4630270302. 7

Teugels, Jozef L. Some representations of the multivariate Bernoulli and binomial distributions, *Journal of Multivariate Analysis*, vol. 32, pp. 256–268, 1990. DOI: 10.1016/0047-259x(90)90084-u. 38, 39, 40, 45

Van Rijsbergen, Cornelius J. *Information Retrieval*, 2nd ed., Butterworths, Boston, 1979. 15

Yu, Clement T., Buckley, C., Lam, K., and Salton, G. A generalized term dependence model in information retrieval, in *Information Technology: Research and Development*, vol 2, pp. 129–154, 1983. 36

Author's Biography

ROBERT M. LOSEE

Robert Losee has been a professor at the University of North Carolina at Chapel Hill's School of Information and Library Science since 1986, after receiving a Ph.D. from the University of Chicago. He has taught courses in Information Retrieval, including an introductory graduate course, and an advanced Artificial Intelligence for Information Retrieval course. He has also taught courses in Information Theory, including a doctoral seminar in the area. His most recent monograph is *Information from Processes: About the Nature of Information Creation, Use, and Representation* (Springer, 2012).

Printed in the United States
by Baker & Taylor Publisher Services